T0123234

Jewel of the South

Civil Rights Biography of Rev. Dr. L.E. Bennett

SHARON K. BENNETT

authorHOUSE®

AuthorHouse™
1663 Liberty Drive
Bloomington, IN 47403
www.authorhouse.com
Phone: 833-262-8899

Published by AuthorHouse 04/17/2024

ISBN: 978-1-6655-6904-0 (sc)
ISBN: 978-1-6655-6903-3 (hc)
ISBN: 978-1-6655-6905-7 (e)

Library of Congress Control Number: 2022915604

*Copyright Registration number: **TXU002224968** 10/19/2020*

Print information available on the last page.

Contents

If you enjoy this book, please take the time to tell us about it. Leave a review on Amazon by scanning the QR Code or your origin of purchase. Thank you very much!

Tribute

Reverend L.E. Bennett: Servant—Mentor—Friend
By
María Antonietta Berriozábal

I met him as Reverend Dr. L.E. Bennett and a group of Baptist Ministers from San Antonio's West End neighborhood. He became one of the leaders in that area to help me address long-standing problems in a very low-income community of San Antonio.

During my tenure as Councilwoman of District 1 (1981 – 1991), West End was one of two neighborhoods in San Antonio with a large concentration of African-Americans. While San Antonio's East Side is known for its significant history of our African-American community, West End also had important African-American history but was not as known. For example, during Reconstruction, blacks moved to two areas - the East Side of today, known then as the Baptist Enclave, and the West End, known as Newcombville after James Pearson, its founder, who was a leader during Reconstruction.

African-Americans established leading churches on the East Side, where they founded major businesses and where black doctors, lawyers, and other professionals set up shop. The first African-American elected and appointed leaders in government and other institutions from their leadership surfaced. While West End also had African-American businesses and professional offices, the area was much smaller.

These facts are essential to the story of Reverend Bennett because instead of serving his community in the East Side, which had more political clout, he chose to pastor in the West End neighborhood, which was home to many low-income and vulnerable families.

The neighborhood needed infrastructure, housing, and services for children and the elderly. It required help calling attention to Lincoln Courts' needs, a public housing project created for African-Americans in West End's midst. However, in time, the project became half Hispanic and half African-American. When I got elected, I discovered that there were no influential community groups who took responsibility for Lincoln Courts. Neither Hispanic/Latino groups nor African-Americans.

When I called together those West End pastors, as I needed much help, Reverend Bennett was one of two pastors who not only attended an organizing meeting that I called, but he became a leader of the faith leaders who took responsibility. He assisted in creating the West End Ministers Alliance, and he became vocal about the needs of that area.

He was a leader among the other pastors and joined other groups working on behalf of the entire West End neighborhood. He was faithful and effective in organizing and attending meetings and press conferences, and he planned many successful efforts that alleviated the needs.

I recall most of Reverend Bennetts positive attitude and smile even with challenging things. He was an exemplary strategist helping me figure out the best path to acquire the city funds needed for infrastructure and other services. In addition, he organized and expertly articulated the needs of his community before the City Council.

Reverend Bennett was a man who did not need to talk about himself. Instead, he concentrated on the needs of others. It was not until after I left City Council that I learned his professional history and distinguished and broad contributions to the civil rights movement in significant ways.

Reverend Bennett worked for civil rights from within his heart and soul. His life was a gift to his community with no need for fanfare.

He was an example of strength and courage shown with authenticity, respect, and deep care for God's vulnerable children. I honor his name and pay tribute to his goodness. He is our hidden jewel of the south.

In my Mexican American culture, we have a way of lifting those no longer with us. So we say *Presenté – Present* because that person will always be with us.

!Reverend Dr. L.E. Bennett, Presenté!
María Antonietta Berriozábal

My Daddy

My father, Rev. Dr. L.E. Bennett, was my hero. Of course, he wasn't famous with tons of people or cameras following him around in Texas, but he was a trailblazer, and his work was necessary. Notoriety and prestige were things for which he didn't care. Daddy only wanted to do the right thing. It took many peoples involvement to transform lives, and there were many unsung heroes with untold stories in U.S. history. For our people, history is everything!

I don't remember much about the civil rights movement. I was only four years old in 1961. I do, however, recall Daddy dressed up or in his work clothes, coming home and leaving a lot. For my siblings and me, the primary care figure was our mother. I recall the sad sentiment and repeated television programs in 1968 of Dr. Martin Luther King's assassination. Unfortunately, my first experience with racism was in the fourth grade; I never forgot my heartbreak when the school principal told me I couldn't represent our school in the citywide Spelling Bee because I was a 'N.' And the trauma of seeing my younger brother receiving a brutal beating from our father because of a lying female neighbor.

I regret my disregard, holding wounds open, waiting to tell his whole story. However, even after becoming engaged in researching family history with him, I self-published a small booklet that mostly contained the Bennett and Jones family trees, along with a photo collection of both families. He refused for me to write certain information citing embarrassment. Though I highlighted my father, it was to have the family records in an easy-to-access format for our legacy. It wasn't until recently that I've come to terms with certain emotions and the time to collect other contributions. Also, when my mother mentioned items in the bottom of his file cabinet after his death, I was shocked at the treasure trove of documents of his accomplishments. The Covid-19 pandemic and restrictions added further delay.

Daddy wasn't perfect, but he didn't need to be. None of us need to be. We need to be braver. Elie Wiesel once said, "We must take sides. Neutrality helps the oppressor, never the victim."

My father was my knight in shining armor, and I love him deeply. Though, if I'm honest, I disliked him and, at times, hated him, he taught me about commitment, respect, loyalty, and love, not necessarily through words but through action. But, unfortunately, there weren't manuals on how to raise children. Back then, parents' only guides were whatever their parents did before them.

Finding the delicate balance of child-rearing was like a physics class. The balance was obtainable yet tricky. You could not use enough teaching and discipline, or your kids may turn out spoiled and weak. However, if one used too much, the child could be resentful and a terror to others. Possibly even hate their parents in their adult life for Lord knows what, or carry things seen through a child's immature lens through to adulthood without discussing the issues.

People filled with loathing and anger took it out on their children. And Bible Thumpers, who swore the Lord intended the rod for harsh treatment. However, if a child was lucky enough to get a loving parent, that was a big piece. Children know and can feel when they're genuinely loved. They will forgive all things when your love and care are real.

My Daddy, the man who finally wasn't too offended to sit and talk with me about my feelings, frustrations, and desires. The one who encouraged me to follow my heart and not be embarrassed by any choice made, as long as I thought it through and was comfortable in it. The man who kissed and hugged me ensured he was always with me, even with the mistake of my getting pregnant before college graduation and the guy turning out to be an irresponsible nutcase.

Daddy was a true man. He was intelligent, kind, strong, a supporter, and a funny guy who loved jokes and music. He was a man of leadership, supporter, provider, and protector and was always there for his family; my father had big eyes, full cheeks, and dimples. I loved his smile, beautiful singing voice, and perfect penmanship.

As the proud daughter of the man this book is about, it's my honor to share with others. I deem the book as my duty. Considering the continuous onslaught of negative media headlines underscoring the continued racial tension in our country—and throughout the world—I don't feel like I have a choice. My father devoted his life and risked everything to fight for equality. Therefore, I intend to fight for equality, share his story, and continue his legacy.

No, I didn't initially appreciate all my father's sacrifices. Yet, I'm very grateful now. But, to me, L.E. Bennett was "Daddy." He was the man who worked every day and made us go to church on Sundays. He disciplined us and fussed but complimented and hugged us.

As a stylish dresser who wanted his family to look sharp, "Appearances are important," he'd say. "How you portray yourself on the outside will inevitably affect how you think about yourself." He was a cool cat.

I desire this book to empower, inspire, and motivate you to make a difference in the world. Any one person can make a difference. According to a Pew study, more than sixty percent of people say they're against prejudice, discrimination, or antagonism directed against someone of a different race, ethnicity, or sexual orientation, not believing theirs is superior. Yet, racism continues.

If my father were still alive, he'd encourage you to take a stance and fight. But, unfortunately, he's not here, so I do this for him. Civil rights aren't about "way back then." They're about right now. Civil rights also aren't about "some people." They're about—and for—all people.

Thank you for showing me what a real man's man was. It's been hard to find another. Thank you for our conversations, the lessons, reconciliation, and understanding. I always feel your spirit around me, and I still hear your voice. I love and miss you, Daddy.

Thank you to the curators of the Bullock Museum in Austin, Texas, for deeming this story worthy enough from their Texas Stories Project and an exhibit.

Peace, Love, and Blessings,
Sharon K. Bennett

**L.E. with Sharon
and Louis>**

**L.E., Sharon and Kenneth
Corpus Christi.(below)**

L.E. and Sharon

San Antonio

Numerous people have documented the first civil rights movement throughout the years. However, despite the bounty of data, many figures and views remain unexplored, especially from the southern states of Texas and Louisiana. Yet, with all the political and civil unrest today, the lessons from that first era are plentiful and can be applied.

San Antonio is a major city in south-central Texas that gained independence from Mexico in 1836. It's beautiful with a sparkling river that winds through town aligned with restaurants, an outdoor theater, museums, and a glass mall. Today it's the seventh most populous city in the United States, second in Texas, with a metropolitan population of over 2,550,000, in 2020 and non-visible racial tension. The U.S. Armed Forces have multiple bases around the city and toots as home to four Fortune 500 companies.

But from the 1950s to the 1960s, the city had persistent segregation and ordinances which corporations continued not to abide. As a result, though believed to be a quiet city without issues, similar to those in states like Mississippi, Arkansas, North Carolina, Kansas, or Tennessee, the Black and Spanish communities were segregated and dissatisfied. Countless white residents didn't care for civil rights but weren't discouraged enough to join the Klu Klux Klan or burn crosses. Instead, they would complain and resist the changes for seats on buses, in theaters, or at restaurant counters.

Overlooking laws regarding the improvement of black lives wasn't unusual. Even with the Civil Rights Act of 1964, racism in employment continued. Daddy fought for the integration of a telecommunications conglomerate and won ahead of the Civil Rights Act signing with Johnson and King. Rev. Dr. L.E. Bennett wasn't always a minister, and thank goodness because he used a few choice words during initial integration meetings.

In my research, there appeared to be latent disrespect or dismissiveness at every turn. I found what Ms. Jacqueline Jones said in her Black Workers Remember article of 2000 to be true. Those corporations didn't care about the black unions nor who their officers or members were. What records they did have were thrown out or burned. They retained very little of the history; unless you were in some significant city followed by tons of members who donated to your funds, which drew national attention.

It was up to family members and friends to share the information. It's shocking how little today the phone company's current Communication Workers of America (C.W.A.) members know or care. I had to quell my disappointment and continue with the mission to tell Daddy's story. The pipelines between black employees at multiple Bell Telephones weren't as well connected nor with as many members as the black sleeping car porters. Yet, it was valuable work that started a chain reaction that needed to happen with this telecommunications conglomerate.

My father fought courageously against injustice and indecency in his quest for equality; this story matters. His work and other great names in the Civil Rights Movement were monumental stepping stones in the right direction. However, modern-day African Americans still face the same underlying negative core values my father stood against, making this a timely and relevant tale for not only Black Americans, but all people who value democracy.

Bennett also uplifted his community by assisting in voter registration as an active worker in the NAACP for years, serving on numerous boards, obtaining funds to get updated plumbing to rehabilitate homes, etc. The man called the "Jewel of the South" by former councilwoman María A. Berriozábal became a minister and earned his doctorate in the late 1980s.

Pushed to his limit, Bennett bore the brunt of insolence, disparaging remarks, arguments, and slurs on his journey for equality. But he persisted, and now he's a prime example of how one person can be a powerful force in ending cycles of inequality, unfairness, and economic disparities. No one was too small to effect change. No one. You can't help but wonder what made people like Martin Luther King, John Kennedy, Malcolm X, Medger Evers, L.E. Bennett, Gates, or Buffets of the world so different.

What made them take up a seemingly impossible challenge? Possibly it was their mindset.

With the on slot of anger and election fraud conspiracy theories, racism has reared its ugly head in the 21ˢᵗ century. People initially denied being racist; however, their verbal responses reeked racial tones and disparities. Irrespective of the facts laid before them, people have unconscious biases. And these hateful occurrences will continue until individuals can open their eyes as a community, a nation, and a human race. Those who had experienced racism recognized these behaviors. Then Former President Donald Trump and varied government officials tried removing or changing voting rights by targeting highly ethnic counties. And local politicians worked to redraw the district lines to account for more seats in the Senate. What needs to be understood is: "We will not go back." People had become so emboldened that their negative and revolting actions led to the nation's capital invasion on January 6, 2021, when the building was closed to tours, killing three and injuring numerous others. The United States is a democracy.

This biography followed my Daddy from humble beginnings as a country kid to a U.S. Army Soldier, to janitor up the social and corporate ladder as a black man in America; his stressors were immense. Bennett acquired commendations and certificates from the NAACP signed by National President Roy Wilkins, Rev. C.D. Owens, and W.C. Patton; presented an award from Wall of Tolerance signed by Rosa Parks; and acquired some media coverage regarding his work and many awards.

Numerous people lost their histories. Multiple loved ones were kidnaped from or near their homes, after leaving for work in the morning, and never returned in the evening. And those brutally beaten, shot, hung, or burned all because of the melanin in their skin. The world must remember their sacrifices and spirit though they've slipped into a book of lost names. These and other injustices dug at L.E.

The youngest of twelve living children, L.E. Bennett, dared to want more. He barely fed his family each payday with the phone company's penance. However, Southwestern Bell/ AT&T didn't allow applications for higher-level positions due to the color of one's skin.

Watching as John F. Kennedy delivered a speech on doing what a person can to uplift themselves and their communities hit home. On

September 12, 1960, in front of the Alamo, in downtown San Antonio, TX, he delivered a speech. At the time, L.E. worked in the offices on Travis street and was on lunch break. Kennedy had made an indelible impression upon him. The charismatic presidential candidate planted a seed that further provoked the young activist to step forward. It has been a revolution indeed. One he initially was glad to engage. This very moment spurred L.E. Bennett to take the lead for workplace impartiality. But the pressures from such a position proved incalculably stressful and harmful.

He wasn't famous, followed in the streets by thousands, or placed in numerous newspapers for headlines. However, he indeed fought for and achieved craft-level integration with the conglomerate Southwestern Bell/AT&T, and his life was at risk during a company convention. L.E. wasn't always a pastor and was a force to be reckoned with, direct and outspoken, didn't mind cursing you when deserved, and now his job security was in jeopardy. Regardless, his wife prepared with a part-time job in case she had to feed their family. Whether people wanted to admit his accomplishments, thank him or not, he did what he did because it was necessary, not for applause.

Angered, L.E. had expressed to his mother that privileged white people undervalued people of color and how he had to control himself from losing his temper. But, as union president, how would he shake things up without risking any small advancements the union had already gained? At that moment, the matriarch gave him a golden nugget to use in his campaign.

However, we're getting ahead of ourselves. You first must know about the origins of L.E. Bennett. What made him the spirited person who took the lead in integration?

1

Amazing Grace

The colorful family he'd been born with was where the saga started. The Bennetts humble beginnings started in Louise, Texas small, dusty southern locale, about one hour west of Houston off Highway-59. A railroad ran through the center of town on a vast dirt road. This was a 1930s country town of poor people with dirt roads, oil wells, and farmlands that provided cotton, dairy, sugar, hay, hogs, and beef.

It had wood-framed buildings with creaky wooden walkways lined on opposite sides of the broad dirt road. Yet, in Louise, all the signs of a well-established small town existed: a grocer, tailor, blacksmith, hardware shop, feed store, hotel, and bar.

On December 4, 1933, a family member summoned Great-Aunt Martha Williams to Daniel (Dan) and Anice Isabell Bennett on a bright and briskly cold night sometime before midnight. A longtime midwife, Martha delivered the Bennetts twelfth and last child, L.E.

The initials did not stand for anything, and no one had explained his name. Many would try to change it. Nevertheless, it remained L.E. written with the periods his entire life.

In some ways, he was a child of promise. His mother's birth pangs started at dusk; nonetheless, his debut didn't occur until the dawning of a new day at 1:00 a.m. on December 4, 1933.

L.E. had nine living siblings, starting with Webb (Buddy), Hattie Mae (Totah), Mack, Carl, Lloyd (Blow), Martha, Norcie (Cout), Ray (Led), and Floyd (Honey). Alzena (baby girl) succumbed at age five from pneumonia.

At four years old, Daniel Lloyd (Sonny) was known as a blue baby who had expired from an asthma attack. All the attention fell on L.E., at least for a while

Daniel (Dan) Bennett stood about 6'4". Early-balding, with broad shoulders, massive muscular arms, a narrow waistline, and curly thick black hair until his 40s. The Bennett boys resembled their father as they grew up: all 6'2" or taller, with broad shoulders, narrow waists, long dark eyelashes, thick dark eyebrows, nicely trimmed mustaches, and clear brown skin. Whenever people witnessed them, they would sheepishly ask, "You are one of Dan Bennetts' boys, ain't ya?" They were popular with the girls, and L.E. was no exception.

Dan's wife, Anice, of average height, boasted a full figure with a smooth mocha complexion, dark grey eyes, long black hair past her shoulders and she always pinned it in a bun at the back or up top. Anice's heritage included African American, Creole, and German.

Anice and Dan raised their children with plenty of affection and a lot of firm discipline. The clan learned to love and respect each other. If a quarrel arose, the children got whipped, then had to hug and kiss—a bitter pill for them to swallow. The kids still disliked each other. The experience taught them that they were brothers and sisters no matter what.

Located on a white man's farm where they sharecropped, an old A-framed red house called "The Red Place" was where the Bennetts resided. The quaint home boasted five rooms, two fireplaces, with front and back porches.

Not rich, Dan and Anice cultivated plenty of heart for all their children. But, still and all, not accepted in the household was nonsense behavior from children.

In those days, no electricity or in-house plumbing existed for the poor. Nevertheless, the Bennetts kept their house neat and clean because Anice insisted everyone got up early each morning and cleaned their rooms, making their beds and sweeping the floor.

The process didn't take long, with the boys in one bedroom and the girls in another. Afterward, Anice would inspect and approve the work. Then, if the children desired to go back to bed on the weekends, they could do so. But unfortunately, they didn't feel like returning to bed after finishing their chores.

Anice did domestic work and attended to her family and home. Though poor with little academics, Anice had a lot of common sense, and her devout Christian principles with great character navigated her life. For example, one of her Christian rituals was that she insisted on prayer before every meal, before bed at night, and rising in the morning.

Anice's deep belief in God and how to raise her children came from her parents. Especially the method of swift discipline. She was not a worldly woman but a superb seamstress, ensuring her family stayed clothed and those garments remained mended.

Dan, a sharecropper and migrant worker with a Work Progress Administration (WPA) program, was a part of the 1935 executive order 8802 by the federal government during F.D. Roosevelt's term.

The order created jobs for men in construction: digging ditches, clearing off the land, cutting down trees or branches, and manually hauling them off thru the worst years of the Depression. Programs even existed involving art and building restoration.

Webb, the eldest child, loved Grandfather John Lloyd's stories and listened to the different languages, including his tribal tongue. John Lloyd was kidnapped from the Ivory Coast of Africa as he fished with his mother for the family's meal. He was thirteen and never returned to the shores he loved. Then, smiling from ear to ear, Webb asked his parents how they met, a story unknown to many. But, Webb said, "In those days, children didn't ask such questions of their parents. Although, Papa told the story one night by the fire."

"Dan dated someone before meeting Anice," Webb said. "Once Dan laid eyes on Anice, mesmerized by her, he fell totally in love. They married in 1911. At sixteen years old, Anice met Dan, twenty-five. When she first became a mother with me, she was seventeen. I was born in 1912."

"No one and no family was perfect," and "I am never ashamed of any family member or their deed." So were the statements Anice made often. Instead, she remained proud and upright.

After supper, the Bennett family sat on the porch while Anice played the guitar and sang Christian songs. If a child neglected to do daily chores, Anice would tell the children a scary story after the singing, and afterward, before preparing for bed, she would firmly remind the shirker of their forgotten chore.

At age five, L.E.'s only chore was to empty the slop jar—which contained human waste—and bring it back before evening to relieve themselves during the night without inside plumbing. One night, L.E. forgot the chore, prompting Anice to tell a story about her childhood, which she started threateningly.

Long ago, her family lived in a small house in the woods in North Texas. A colossal tree grew at an angle near the kitchen window. One evening, as the family gathered for the meal, they prayed and talked about their day. Suddenly, an animal growled from outside. Anice peered out and spied a lion on its thick bottom branch with his front paws crossed and his head positioned on them. The lion glared at them as they ate. Anice screamed. Her father snatched his gun and ran the cat off.

The lion may have been waiting outside his home, so L.E. was now afraid to do his chore late at night. The five-year-old stood at the door trying to peer into the darkness; his heart beat faster, and his legs trembled. He gazed pleadingly into his mother's eyes.

"Well, go on! The slop jar ain't gonna walk in here to ya," Anice said.

L.E. raced to the outhouse, grabbed the slop jar, and shot back. Anice laughed, hugged him, and sent him to bed. She made up the story to scare him, but it worked. After that, the boy would never forget his chores again.

The Bennett siblings sat around to tell more about their parents and child-rearing. Knowing Anice and Dan helped explain who they were in life. Delving in more exhibited their character and L.E.'s beliefs. "Are you prepared to meet your maker? Because if Dan Bennett said he's going to do something, you could believe it!"

Firstly, Dan Bennett didn't smile much, and people respected him for keeping his word. He was a formidable adversary. Second, Dan, the breadwinner, was responsible for feeding his family. One winter, the food—and money—were running low, so Dan went to see the area grocer, Mister Ward.

"Mister Ward, I'm a need sum things on credit agin'. Now, I always pay ya my debts, and I will agin', soon as I get sum work in the spring. But, now, I gotta feed my family."

"Dan, I know ya a man of ya word, but I also need my money. I just can't wait that long for ya to pay."

"Mister Ward, my word is my bond. I don't care if I go hungry, but

I'm not gonna let my kids starve. I'm a need flour, sugar, and beans, and I'm a pay ya soon as I get sum money."

"Dan, I just can't! Times is hard for everybody. If'n ya need anythin', ya gonna have to pay for it."

"I tell ya what, Mister Ward, I'm a walk over there and get the flour, sugar, and beans. And I hope ya don't try ta stop me. I'm a pay ya when I can."

Dan pulled a potato sack from his back pocket, selected the groceries, thanked Mister Ward, and left. Afterward, he tied the loaded bag to his saddle, hopped on the horse, and headed home. But, having known Dan for years, Mister Ward didn't notify the police, and, come spring, he got his money.

Dan was well-known in the region as an honest man. He and his cousin first arrived in Louise on horseback. A wooden sign nailed to a sizable tree read, "Run Negro Run, and if ya can't read, run anyway." First caught their eye. Somebody had etched a black stick figure of a person running into the sign. Dan wrapped a rope around it, drug it down, and the handmade sign never got replaced.

The people of this small town got along well, with minimal outside influences, such as the Ku Klux Klan (KKK) coming through to abduct or kill Negros. One summer day, a lousy rumor reached Anice's ears.

"If you disagree with your spouse and think they cheated, get your rifle and go for what you know." It was a phrase the siblings sang out as they divulged one of the following stories. The meaning of the statement became clear as I listened.

The horrendous scandal that a woman and Dan had messed around in the woods had circled. Nevertheless, true or not, Anice did not want such stories spread around town about her family, ruining their reputation. So Anice marched up the dirt road through town to handle her business. Finally, she arrived at the woman's paint-worn white gate, leaned on the old fence, tried to catch her breath, and called the woman out.

"Ms. Shaker, it's Mrs. Bennett. Can I speak ta ya, please?"

Ms. Shaker approached her front screen door wearing a dingy white under-slip, smoking a cigarette. She removed the cigarette from her mouth, leaned on the doorframe, and with a flippant tone, asked, "What?"

Anice scoffed, "I need ta talk with ya, so ya chil'ren don't hea' me."

5

Ms. Shaker snatched a thin housecoat with a floral print and came out. The dirty screen door creaked as it slammed closed behind her. Ms. Shaker sashayed out to the gate. Then, smirking, she announced, "What?"

Anice yanked the woman's hair and beat her face and body without another word.

Ms. Shaker started wailing and ended up on the ground.

Frowning and biting her bottom lip as she pointed her finger at the woman, Anice said, "I betta, not evah hea' such a story again, and ya don't evah disrespect me." Then, with a scowl, she turned and marched back past the town, kicking up dust before returning home to prepare the family's meal.

The Sun was beginning to set as Dan entered the door from work. Anice was sitting at the hefty wooden table, loading her rifle. Dan stopped just inside the front door and glared at Anice. Dan and Anice were hunters and excellent marksmen who could hit a target. They each owned a 30-30 rifle.

"So, ya think ya gonna make a fool of me, Negro?"

"Gal, what ya talking 'bout? Is ya crazy?"

Next, Anice loaded his rifle, stood, and threw it at him. She pointed her gun at Dan and stipulated, "Negro, ya will not disrespect me. Now, go for what ya know."

Dan unloaded and tossed his rifle over on the sofa. "No, Gal."

Anice moved from behind the table, walked over to him, looking up forcefully, and she said, "I betta, not evah hea' anythin' like that a'gin. True or not. Ya hea' me?"

She subsequently placed her rifle on the table and went to bed. The rumors quickly stopped and didn't arise again during their lifetimes.

With my head tilted and brow furrowed, I asked my Uncle why his parents used such derogatory pet names. The N-word, no less! It seemed harsh and unloving to me, yet, they were anything but that with each other.

Webb rubbed his chin. Wide-eyed as if searching the air for an answer, he exhaled sharply, "You know what, niece? They never explained. As the eldest, I've never heard them call each other anything else." Paused for a moment, he snapped his fingers, "Ooh, except that one sad time. You'll soon know when."

Ill-advisedly, Anice did pay another visit to Ms. Shaker, whose daughters had been pushing and pulling on Martha's and Norcie's hair at school. So Anice made a second and last visit to Ms. Shaker. Anice left the children playing in the yard, marched back through town, and leaned on the same old fence, catching her breath. But, alas, she called for Ms. Shaker to come out.

Ms. Shaker arrived at the door, "Yes, Mrs. Anice?"

Anice asked Ms. Shaker if she wanted her butt whipped again. Ms. Shaker declined, and the Bennett girls never had another problem.

The towns chatter about these antics of the two women spread like wildfire. But Anice didn't care. Melvin was born a few months before Webb (Buddy), half-sibling of the Bennett children.

Dan was remarkably kind to Anice and the children. He was an excellent protector and provider. There were times when Anice didn't get up early on weekend mornings and slept longer than usual. Dan didn't wake her or allow the kids to either. He recognized she needed rest, and it's what she got. Anice and Dan taught their kids and grandchildren pride, responsibility, and good temperament.

Amazing Grace (2nd verse, Anice Bennett)

"Amazing Grace, how sweet the sound, that saved a wretch like me, I once was lost, but now I'm found. I was blind, but now I see.

'I was young, but I recall that singing was Mother's joy and the shadows of the workers that would gather at the close of day.

As I sat on my mother's knee in those days that used to be, it was there that she taught me all about God's amazing Grace.'

Amazing Grace, how sweet the sound. That saved a wretch like me-e-e."

Anice Bennett, L.E' 's mother, wrote her second verse to "Amazing Grace." His mother's rendition still caused tears to swell up in his eyes. To Anice, as the sunset at the end of a workday, she would see the workers' shadows as they traveled home.

Church on Sundays continued to be mandatory in the Bennett household. A tradition L.E. devoutly repeated with his own family. In addition, L.E. used his smooth tenor voice boastfully in any choir.

As an adult, he participated in the church's men's choir; L.E. also wrote songs and poetry. In late 1955, he penned a song for his future wife, Essie Jones. He mailed the tune to various artists, such as Nat King Cole and

Frank Sinatra, hoping to add the ballad to their repertoire. Years later, he listened to a Sinatra song with similar lyrics. At first offended, confident it was indeed his melody, which he never got paid for, but the number never caught on. Although, L.E. suggested that the piece would have been a hit if Frank had sung the track correctly.

L.E. kept this song and poems in a huge old brown duffel bag with letters he'd received concerning his civil rights activities, a variable treasure trove. One such letter arrived from Robert Kennedy. But, those papers were for his eyes only, so he stored them in the attic of the first tiny home leased with his wife.

He'd forgotten the duffel bag during a move, with everything going on with his life in a rush. The new tenants disposed of the case before L.E. returned to reclaim his attaché. Such a loss broke his heart. After losing so many uncopied songs and poems, he never regained that same inspiration to resume writing songs or poetry again. However, I believe his active life with civil rights is where his passion transitioned. The numerous letters and sermons that he penned took center stage.

Also, L.E. possessed the ability to take the complicated and make it simple. He reviewed all the facts and thought of options. Once he decided on a choice, he developed the steps and followed that plan until the end. He was direct, concise, and determined. If a way existed to make a complex problem more tolerable, people handed the issue over to L.E. He found a way to reduce it to a simple form and got maximum results. He comes to use this skill in civil rights and managing a church.

A very complex, industrious man who read regularly, and L.E. listened intently. He said, "The important parts were in the details." When doing business, he was all business; conversely, during fun, he emerged in fun. To peer into who L.E. Bennett was means understanding more about his history.

Do You Know Me?

My heart, my soul, my spirit?
Who am I to you or myself?

Who am I? What am I? Am I beautiful because I have
socially acceptable features by man's account, or am
I beautiful because I love myself and others?
I am a seeker through this place we call earth.
What I seek is a higher plane.
A spiritual understanding. A place where we aid
each other with no thought of repayment.

Do you listen as I speak?
Do you hear my heart as it cries out?
Do you know me?

Sharon Bennett 2003

2

Childhood Jealousy

Growing up, the family showered L.E. with love and attention. His sisters fussed over him, always playing with his long, curly black locks like his father and grandfather's hair. Dan brought something home from work for L.E., the youngest boy, and Martha, the youngest girl. The family called L.E. *Baby* even after walking, talking, and running.

While Anice was gone to town one spring day, L.E.'s mischievous nature got him. While the other children were playing outside, he planned to climb onto the china cabinet and get a small "Texas Jack" knife. Anice had previously warned him not to touch the blade; L.E. saw the shiny red blade at the top of the cabinet. And with the help of a chair, he accomplished his mission.

L.E. ran outside to show his siblings his newest possession. The other kids froze in place, eyes wide and mouths gaped open. The children understood not to play with knives, especially six-year-old Baby. Ray laid chase to retrieve the cutter, but Baby ran, holding the blade. An old tattered mattress with exposed springs lay in the yard, and Baby tripped over it. He fell; the edge went straight through his tongue. Blood gushed everywhere, and L.E. screamed bloody murder.

Norcie and Martha perceived their punishment would be brutal and swift if they revealed Baby's escapade to their parents—it would mean sure death to them all. While their parents were away, the older children were responsible for them. In those days, if one got punished, all got punished. So they kept giving him water to rinse out his mouth, and every time he raised the glass to his mouth, the water turned bright red. The bleeding eventually stopped. Alternately, the ordeal was far from over.

Anice returned home and saw Baby's mouth swollen, plus he had trouble speaking. The children told Anice what happened when she returned, and not only did L.E.'s butt hurt, but his tongue also had a problem. The worst thing about the spanking was that he couldn't even cry right because of the injury to his mouth. Ray was also severely chastised and whipped for making his brother run and fall.

A few days later, still sore from the double chastisement of scolding and whipping, Ray decided to get back at his little brother. He enticed Baby to the side of the house to play barbershop, out of the other's view. Ray cut clumps of curly hair off L.E.'s head to ensure their sisters would no longer swoon over L.E.'s thick black hair.

Ray concluded that giving the extreme haircut was worth being on the receiving end of Anice's wrath later in the day. He got all that was coming to him after the clip job. L.E. shook off the experience; he still thought he might get away with anything, even if it annoyed his brothers and sisters.

Every member of the Bennett household had a designated spot in the table's vast kitchen/living area. However, after the older four children married and left home, Anice redid the seating assignment. Next, only a couple of months later, the six-year-old tried another stunt.

Anice and Dan each sat at opposite ends of the table. Baby understood his spot was to the left of Anice, and one evening when his brother Lloyd came for dinner, Baby sat in his brother's seat. Lloyd asked him to get up, except Baby wanted to sit differently, and he sat in Lloyd's chair.

Irritated, Lloyd moaned, "Momma, Baby won't get out of my seat."

"Don't worry, I'll handle it," she responded.

Calmly Anice continued to fix the plates for dinner. Afterward, she quietly walked outside and got a switch from a small tree. The minute she returned to carry out her task, Baby jumped up and ran out of the house. One thing Anice hated was for a child to run when she would whip you. Still, she closed in and got a few licks.

"Don't ya run from me, boy," Anice shouted as L.E. jetted out and around the side of the house.

"Baby, get back here!"

He rounded the house for the third time and received another stroke.

Baby glanced up and surveyed his Papa's tall, broad-shouldered silhouette coming down the farm road in the setting sun.

Only he can save me from this terrible whipping, Baby thought. So he ran for him, screaming, "Papa! Papa!"

Dan picked up Baby, glad he was enthusiastic to see his father. Baby's refuge in his father's arms was but for a moment. Anice soon appeared with a scowl on her face.

"Put 'em down, 'N,'" Anice demanded, panting and sweating.

"What's the baby dun', Gal?" Dan asked.

"I said, put 'em down, 'N,'" she repeated. "I'm not through with 'em yet."

Dan lowered Baby cautiously to the ground. His son couldn't believe Papa would let her whip him. L.E. had yet to learn about the woman of the house. Anice lashed Baby back home.

They all returned to the dinner table; there were tears in Baby's eyes and whip marks on his legs and arms. The waiting family had washed their faces and hands. When Anice was ready, they said a prayer, and ate dinner. The siblings dared not ask any questions about what had happened.

That evening marked a change in L.E.'s treatment. The exceptional attention and coddling paid to him were over. From then on, Anice disciplined him like the rest of the children.

When I Was Young

Growing long, tall, and thin, I would reminisce on
Momma's guiding hand when I was young.
She walked, talked, and prayed with me so my soul would not be lost.
To her, I owe it all. I can never pay the cost. She's the gleam in my eyes,
And the light in my heart.
Dear Lord, I pray, please, that we should never part!

Sharon Bennett October 2000

3

Big Loss

Dan's job with the WPA involved clearing trees from the land. He and another worker, Mr. Kuntz, cut the trees with a two-person crosscut saw and carried the pieces to the pickup area. Awkwardly, Mr. Kuntz's legs gave way while the two men hauled a tree trunk. Dan was left to transport it by himself, a tremendous weight on him.

Approximately three weeks later, Dan grimaced and complained to Anice about chest pain. Ultimately, Dan rose, drank some coffee on the third morning, kissed his wife goodbye, and left. He headed up the same dirt road he took every morning, down a trail, across the creek, and through a path in the woods.

The children took the same route to school each morning. Martha, Lloyd, and Floyd were walking to school down the wooded path when they came across their dad, leaning back against a tree with his legs stretched across the trail. Although, to the kids, he appeared to be sleeping, on the contrary, he'd entered his eternal rest. The children ran back to the house to get Norcie, who told Anice what they'd seen.

Anice raced to check on Dan, who had told her he had experienced chest pain and trouble breathing for two or three days. Sorry to say, nothing Anice could do would save his life. There was no autopsy, but the cause written on the death certificate was heart failure. Dr. Bauknight, the area physician, told the family he believed the cause of demise was a small and slow-growing thoracic aortic aneurysm. Such aneurysms don't permanently rupture, but, for Dan, it had. On January 3, 1940, the

Bennett patriarch slowly bled out without even knowing it. He was forty-one years old.

Anice cleansed her husband's body on the kitchen table as she sang to him, kissed his face, and whispered, "My loving Dan."

The older children helped dress their father in his suit. They later placed him on their parents' bed and covered him with a white sheet. Finally, Anice went to prepare herself for bed. She would lay with her husband for the last time.

Once they prepared the body and placed it in the bed, six-year-old L.E. walked into the darkened room with only the flicker from a lantern where his Papa lay. L.E. called him yet got no response. Finally, Anice told L.E. his Papa had died; but he didn't fully understand. His Papa's body was still on the bed like it always had. Maybe Papa was just asleep, the Baby resolved.

L.E. approached the bed and whispered, "Papa, are ya gonna wake up?" Then, he pulled the sheet back with his small shaking hands and glared at the massive form from head to toe.

"Papa, I love ya," L.E. said while touching his father's hard, cold face. Baby placed the sheet back up over his Papa's face and cried. Numerous crying spells ensued. L.E. never got over the pain and longing for his father.

Uncle Harvey, Anice's brother, made the funeral arrangements. He took his six-wheeled old truck into Wharton to pick up a simple pine casket. On the way back, L.E. and Ray rode in the back of the pickup truck with it.

They held a somber funeral at the country church a few days later. A great man had died while working, trying to earn a living for his wife and children, whom he dearly loved. "Dan was a man among men, and he always went the last mile for you," the reverend said in his eulogy.

Anice carried the heavy load of raising children during a time of hardship. Dan's death had left an irreplaceable void in their hearts forever.

After Dan died, the country continued into World War II. Times were becoming extremely hard for everyone, both whites and blacks. Anice had to make changes to survive. She moved from the country, where she had lived the life of a sharecropper's wife, into town. She plied her trade as a seamstress, cook, and housekeeper for wealthier white families. Anice had six of the dozen children with her. The four eldest had married, and two had died young.

Dan and Anice had done their best to raise their children in a disciplined, Christian manner, so they survived the harsh injustices. Even after Dan's death, attending church was mandatory as long as you lived under Anice's roof.

Every Sabbath started with Sunday school, followed by church services. By the afternoon, it was sweltering. No air conditioners existed—just the church ladies' fans, and they were not enough. Baby sweated and squirmed on the hard pew, and the church ladies sang and shouted thanks to God. Baby loved to heed Anice singing in the adult choir, especially when she joined in "Amazing Grace." The Lord had blessed her with a glorious contralto voice. She also directed the youth choir.

There were many singers in the family, as well as ministers. His mother is where L.E. got his voice and love of song. He would sing along from the pew and do his preaching. He loved watching the pastor and his mannerisms.

Some Sundays after services, the church hosted dinner on the grounds. Every mother brought food. The kids played, the ladies gossiped, and the men told tall tales while pitching horseshoes or playing cards. They represented a time of enjoying life, and people could socialize.

Once it came time to eat, the kids would go through the line first and pick foods based on who had cooked them. Parishioners could hear the kids whispering amongst themselves.

A teen boy whispered, "I don't want any of the green beans that sister so-and-so brought. They never really taste like green beans."

His friend grinned and responded, "Boy, you ever ate Sister Smith's meatloaf? Man, it will have you howling at the moon."

On Sundays, there was no such thing as lunch. Alternatively, you ate breakfast before leaving home, attended church all day, and had dinner on the grounds. Then, as the evening set in, everyone bid each other goodnight and went home.

Don't Forget It, Or Else You'll Repeat It

Know your history and from whence you came.
Don't forget it, or else you'll repeat it.
Life is good, and blessings are plentiful. But has the struggle ended?
Don't forget, or else you'll repeat it.

Do you smile in someone's face and spite them behind their back?
Do you scorn your child because they're close
to someone of a different race?
An ignorant racist is not always white, and a dumb N* is
not always black. Don't forget it, or else you'll repeat it.

We still have a long way to go to get a level playing field
Don't forget it, or else you'll repeat it.
Many have died for the cause of civil rights: blacks, Jews, and whites.
Our histories are rich and must stay alive
Don't forget it, or else
You'll repeat it.

Sharon Bennett 1997

Anice Bennett

ANNICE I. BENNETT, HER LATE 30's

Dan Bennett—Children's commissioned rendition

18

Bennett Ladies

Norcie Bennett Barnes

Norci Bennett Barnes

Hattie Bennett Williams (Totah)

Martha Bennett Taylor

Webb (Buddy)   **Mack**   **Carl**

Lloyd   **Floyd**   **Ray, Sr.**

Ray, Carl, Webb, L.E., Floyd   **Melvin, half-sibling**

L.E. Bennett (15)

School Pic (16)

At brotherMack's
in Houston (17)

Houston (19-20)

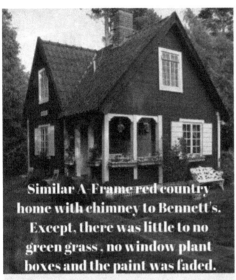

Similar A-Frame red country home with chimney to Bennett's. Except, there was little to no green grass , no window plant boxes and the paint was faded.

Lloyd	Norcie	Martha

Bennett Table

Dan PaPa Bennett

Mama Locke Bennett

Floyd	Bay	L. E.

Dinner table seat assignments

Similar wooden table, chairs & floor to Bennett household

4

Youth's Innocence

"Oh, no! He's going to shoot me," L.E. squealed, jumped up, and ran.

The fall season after his father's death, L.E. started school a year later than usual because of his December birthdate. He would prove to be an exceptional student, but the distance to school was too far for his age to walk.

For children of color, the county didn't provide buses. So L.E. walked while white children rode in the rusty old buses and taunted the walkers. Thenceforth, angrily, L.E. would pick up rocks and throw them toward the bus. Of course, he didn't hit them, but it was a way to let off frustration.

The other Bennett siblings, Lloyd, Norcie and Floyd, had to drop out of school to help Anice pay bills. Therefore, they worked cleaning houses, yards, and picking cotton. Naturally, L.E. wanted to help, and he often rode on his sister Norcie's sack. She secretly hoped a worm would fall on the bag; L.E. would see it, shriek, and run back to the turn-row. But unfortunately, L.E. didn't like worms.

Although it was not L.E.'s forte, many families made considerable money in the fields. Since the others were working, the mantle for a complete education fell on him. But L.E. whined to Anice that he didn't want to go to school; he wanted to work as his brother and sisters did.

To help L.E. feel better about not working and losing his father, Anice took him to the movies one day. The nearest theater was ten miles away in El Campo, Texas. Her brother Harvey gave them a ride both ways.

The town had erected a large tent in a nearby field. A cowboys and

Indians movie showed, and the mothers sat near the back. Sadly, the film was too realistic for young L.E.

"Oh, no! He's going to shoot me," L.E. squealed as he jumped out of his seat and ran toward the exit.

As L.E. ran by, Anice grabbed the troubled child and comforted him, gently explaining that the cowboy on his horse wasn't pointing the gun at him. It was only make-believe. Still, L.E. watched the rest of the film from his mother's lap.

L.E. attended the third through fifth grades in El Campo, Texas, where his mother moved into a small yellow house after Dan's death. But Anice believed L.E. might get a better education in San Antonio. So in 1946, his sister Norcie took him to San Antonio to live with her for the sixth through ninth.

Initially, the San Antonio school administration wouldn't enroll him until he had a real name. So Norcie gave him the name Lee Ernest. The school in San Antonio was a fertile field for L.E.—who had grown to be 6'2" and was still slender. He could never get enough of the classroom experience.

L.E. discovered that he possessed a photographic memory. Hence, anything he read (or even listened to) he remembered. Course work came easy for him, but there was always an overriding mission other than simply learning. L.E. determined a formal education would help him achieve more, and he wanted frantically to do something to help bring some joy into his mother's life.

In his eyes, Anice was the world. She was a beautiful, brilliant woman who labored hard to provide for her children, although she bore the heartache of a deceased spouse and two dead children. Nevertheless, it meant everything for at least one of her children to graduate high school.

Anice worked tirelessly during L.E.'s junior and senior years to ensure he had everything the other school children had. Her little feet would swell from working long hours, and her body ached. But, she wanted L.E.'s education to culminate with him in their auditorium, with his head held high and hers as high as the other parents.

To help his sister Norcie's household, L.E. worked various summer jobs before his freshman year in 1948. He tried picking cotton for two weeks and even picked 205 pounds one day, but he still didn't like it. Cotton seemed pretty, soft, and white from afar, but the bolls grew hard and sharp, ripping minor cuts into fingers that bleed and cause pain. So L.E. sought other work opportunities.

In 1949, the summer after his first year, L.E. went to Houston to spend his vacation with Mack. He expected to gain employment in a major city other than picking cotton. Instead, L.E. acquired a job as a busboy at a local restaurant. The ad in the newspaper asked for bussers, stating they'd be paid salary and tips.

So, when cleaning the tables, L.E. and the other bussers took the money. The situation became a problem because the waitresses were to get the change. L.E. observed injustice, so he organized the workers, and the boss agreed to a meeting.

L.E. told the manager, "The ad is a false advertisement to entice workers."

The supervisor said, "The waitresses are to collect the tips and split them with their busboy."

L.E. stated, "There's no way to guarantee how much they'll collect from the tables or if the waitresses will split them with us. And the best time to explain had been when you interviewed us."

L.E. suggested the bussers' picket against the restaurant. However, not everyone wanted to align with L.E., and he felt disenchanted with his first failed attempt at equality.

So L.E. quit the job and joined the NAACP. A few other boys walked out in solidarity. The budding activist had his path set.

L.E. returned to San Antonio to live with his sister Norcie and her husband, Quinnice. He found summer employment at Sommers Drug Store as a short-order cook and busboy. This steady job enabled him to buy clothes and other items a young man needed. But, despite no segregation laws, blacks weren't allowed to sit at the lunch counters.

L.E. enjoyed San Antonio and found it a premier city to live. There was something special for him about San Antonio's people, climate, flavor, and ethnic makeup. The mix just seemed to say, "We are family." Yet, despite its beauty, San Antonio did not escape racial prejudice. Instead, it hovered like a dark cloud.

According to various online sites like Census.gov and Wikipedia, San Antonio had a total population of over two-million five-hundred thousand people, with 91.3% of Mexican origin, more than 54% of the overall population being Hispanic Tejano, and less than 7% African-American. Yet, in the 1960s, the metropolitan city boasted over five-hundred eighty-seven thousand, with less than 8% being Blacks. Still a far cry from the thirty-four blacks and four-hundred and fourteen Mulattos in 1792.

Even though whites weren't a majority in San Antonio's population, whites had used various tactics, including militias, political offices, and legislation, to re-establish political and social supremacy throughout the South. As a result, African Americans in San Antonio were poorly represented and were politically disenfranchised. Many claimed that San Antonio wasn't as bad as other cities with low violence, but the fact remains that it was segregated and continued to be known as a Sundown town.

One Saturday afternoon in the summer of 1950, sixteen-year-old L.E. planned to go to the movies at the State Theater, located in the Stowers Furniture building on Main and East Houston in downtown San Antonio. The "colored section" of the theater was on the third-floor balconies. While watching the movie, L.E. was eating a Hershey's candy bar. A piece lodged in his throat, and he began to cough. Tactlessly, there were no restrooms or fountain facilities in the colored section. Toilets for colored patrons were on the first floor. As a result, L.E. walked the stairs, all the while choking.

He tried desperately to dislodge that chunk of candy and get air into his lungs. Lastly, L.E. started to feel dizzy and worried he might black out. But he tried not to panic.

L.E. finally made it to the water fountain, took a few sips, dislodged the chewy wad, and wiped his face with a wet handkerchief. No longer gagging or coughing, but he was angry. Why did he need to travel so far for water at the colored fountain to avoid choking to death?

L.E. felt theaters should lower ticket prices for sitting in the colored section. What an inconvenience. For a business to treat you like less than human and, in addition, make you pay for the privilege, L.E. believed, was utterly ridiculous.

L.E. vowed to himself: *I will never go to another theater that compromised my safety.* The theater incident made him so keenly aware of being treated differently. Sure, the lunch counter at Sommers segregated whites, and the people of color had to get their food and leave. However, L.E. didn't see any mistreatment. Now, in the theater, he became painfully aware of the consequences of racism.

After the movie fiasco, L.E. hopped the bus home and headed toward the back. Blacks could pay at the front and walk the aisle to the back of the bus. Getting off and returning through the back door wasn't required. Another colored gentleman who also boarded sat about midway. At the next stop, a white gentleman got on the bus. White people were in all the seats from the front to the midpoint. The driver told the man of color to give him his spot.

The man yelled back, "Go to Hell!"

The white man became furious. A fight ensued, and the man of color pulled a knife. Luckily, other passengers interceded and stopped the fight. The black gentleman stayed in his seat.

In the early 1900s through to the 1920s, mob violence and lynchings existed in San Antonio aimed at local colored and Mexican residents. It was considered their modi operandi.

Based on the number of racist incidents he had seen that summer. L.E. figured it would be best to finish his sophomore through senior years in El Campo, near his mother. The social injustices were all more than he could stomach.

As far as affairs of the heart go, L.E. had his share. The first was a girl by the name of Zara. L.E. was twelve years old, and she was one grade ahead of him. They passed notes to each other through a mutual friend named Ernestine Boston. The two kept Ernestine busy moving messages from Ms. "Short" Anderson's homeroom to Ms. "Tall" Anderson's class. The students nicknamed their teachers because their heights differed while sharing the same last name.

One day as L.E. sat in class, Ernestine passed a note from Zara. He read it and stuck it inside his desk, but Ms. "Short" Anderson saw him and asked if he had put a note in his desk.

L.E. replied, "No, ma'am."

She asked a student next to him if he had seen L.E. put a note inside his desk.

"Yes, ma'am."

As punishment, Ms. "Short" Anderson told L.E. to read the note aloud, which he did. The embarrassment curtailed the note-sending.

L.E. and his lush, curly black baby hair would attract many female admirers throughout the years, except the fathers of these girlfriends objected to any serious courting.

During his sophomore year at E.A. Greer High School, Alma Charleston, a classmate, was L.E.'s romantic interest. Like many before, Alma tried to teach L.E. to play the piano, except he wasn't interested in music beyond trying to sing.

He was, however, a gifted athlete, participating in basketball and football. Sorry to say, while Coach McIntosh was a wonderful person, he knew little about the game. He was a general studies teacher, not athletic, and he didn't even know the proper way to wear the protective pads. Nevertheless, L.E. helped develop most of his team's plays, and the Coach was grateful for L.E.'s assistance.

Alma had a babysitting job after school for a white family. To spend more time with Alma, L.E. decided to escort her to work one day. Unfortunately, in line with the time, Alma's father didn't allow her to date, so L.E. waited up in Ox Blood, a tiny section of town where black folk congregated for fun times.

Many of the juke joints were in Ox Blood. As they walked through the white neighborhood, a woman came to her front door with a German shepherd. Opening the door, she deliberately sicced the dog on Alma and L.E. Seeing the dog approach, growling, and barking, Alma started to run.

L.E. grabbed her by the arm and sternly uttered, "No. Stand still." He remembered his mother telling him never to run from a dog because it would tear him to pieces. L.E. held firm staring into the dog's eyes, not exhibiting any fear, and the dog stopped. After seeing no injury or distress, the white woman called her dog back after a few moments. L.E. nodded at Alma, and she nodded back in recognition. He and Alma continued on their way.

Reflecting on this incident, L.E. declared, "Life will never be at its best in America until we can meet each other on equal ground and treat each other as fellow travelers. I can't help but wonder how delusions in a person's head make them think they're better than another. Some people thought they had the right to rule or had dominion over another. To exact persecution and sadistic harm upon another, in the name of what they dare call some form of Christian righteousness, was the lowest form of human behavior."

L.E. was proud of his striking appearance. As a teen, he considered himself very cute for a valid reason. L.E. felt that he could date any girl he wanted. However, during his senior year, he and some friends attended a girls' basketball game at E.A. Greer High School. L.E. was wearing his blue and gold letter jacket, so there would be no misunderstanding about who he was: quarterback and captain of the football and basketball teams.

He saw a cute light-skinned junior playing center named Essie L. Jones. After the game, L.E. decided to approach her for a date. He was popular and suave, and no one had rejected him—yet.

He commented, "You're good with that ball; with a grin and a lick of his top lip, he commented, "You're good with that ball. Would you like to go out?"

Looking L.E. up and down and assessing his line, Essie Jones snapped back, "Hmmph, get lost!" At that moment, she turned around and ran to the locker room.

L.E.'s eyes bulged, and his mouth fell open, "Wow!" At that point, he left the gym and went home.

Graduation day arrived for L.E. and the E.A. Greer class of 1953. Still known as Baby, Anice's son would graduate with honors as valedictorian. He was a sharp-looking senior, dressed in a black, white shirt with French cuffs, silk socks, and shiny black shoes. Anice was so proud of L.E. that she might burst.

L.E. loved to dress up, which meant a suit, a long-sleeve starched shirt, a designed tie, and cuff links. He believed that if about your business, you should look the part. L.E.'s suits were generally black, brown, tan, navy, and dark green. Setting it off with a mixed-colored tie was fun for him. His other loves were to wear hats and shiny patent leather shoes—never jeans or sneakers.

He would sing "The Other Side of the Mountain" by Arthur Prysock at that night's events, scheduled to be a soloist. The lyrics are about a boy and a girl who will miss happiness because they live on opposite sides of a mountain.

L.E. had that Billy Eckstine type of tenor to his voice. His crooning would give all the girls goosebumps. He worked hard that day, practicing with the music teacher, Mrs. Baker.

There had always been a high school teacher that made all the boys crazy or all the girls go gaga. Mrs. Baker was one of those. A lovely, brown-skinned woman made the boys' hearts pitter-patter when she walked by them.

Graduation evening progressed beautifully, the momentum building and anticipation running wild. Finally, at last, all would hear L.E.'s beautiful voice. The curtains opened, and L.E. stood center stage, sharp and ready to deliver like Eckstine.

Mrs. Baker hit the piano key, and the spotlight illuminated L.E., but when he opened his mouth to croon that lovely song, something came out that he'd never heard. His voice was beyond tenor or baritone. It was more like the cry of a banshee. His friends almost laughed themselves to death.

L.E. managed to survive the embarrassment and complete the song, scratching and screeching the whole way through. But it was a complete disaster. Despite the flop at such a pivotal moment, L.E. continued. Nevertheless, the evening was still a milestone L.E. would cherish.

As the announcer called out L.E.'s name, recognizing him as valedictorian of the Class of 1953, L.E. strutted across the stage, proudly wearing his blue and gold letter jacket under his half-zipped graduation gown. He gave a short speech and humbly accepted the first diploma as a member of the Bennett family during the processional.

Anice Bennett stood up to clap and scream. She cried tears of joy with swollen feet and circles under her eyes. When L.E. received his degree, it was for him and his parents, brothers, and sisters. Anice pulled the rabbit out of a hat.

L.E. knew his father was looking down on them, saying, "Gal, you did it again. I knew you would."

Anice was one unique and beautiful person who always had the answers to life's most challenging problems. She gave all of herself to the well-being of her children.

5

America's Army

In the summer of 1953, L.E. entered the army. America started the Korean War in June 1950 after North Korea invaded South Korea. The military took plenty of young men to build up their troops. Once again, although treated as second-class citizens in the U.S., black Americans would fight in a war for their country. Most Americans fought one battle; African Americans dealt with two: against Communism abroad and bigotry and injustice in the United States.

Nineteen at graduation, L.E. registered with the Armed Services at eighteen, as required by law, due to his late school start. Military tests with examinations set in Houston. Things went off without a problem. L.E. felt grown-up and proud to assist his mother financially, as she'd done for him throughout his life. It's his turn to give back in a big way, and he couldn't wait to see other parts of the world besides Texas.

On test day, eighty-four other young Americans of varying ethnicity waited. Four men scored high enough for Officer Candidate School (O.C.S.) of those taking the test. Three were white, but only one was a man of color named L.E. Bennett.

However, L.E. elected not to pursue O.C.S. and shipped out to Fort Sam Houston Army Base in San Antonio. He finished paperwork, was vaccinated and was sworn into the U.S. Army. Afterward came transportation to Camp Roberts in the San Joaquin Valley of California. He spent sixteen weeks in basic training. Then, again, the command approached him about considering O.C.S. L.E. agreed to the interview process this time but also decided not to accept the opportunity. He wasn't interested and believed it wasn't a war in which Blacks should participate.

When L.E. reflected on the situation, he admitted saying no to O.C.S. had been a mistake but one of the many he would make in life. Even at his interview for O.C.S., not sure why he refused the offer. He recalled the rumors, "A second lieutenant's life wouldn't be worth a plugged nickel in Korea." With Korea as his destination and possibly where his life could have ended in a leadership position. He also didn't like the strict regimentation that accompanied O.C.S.

L.E.'s unit commanding officer for basic training was First Lieutenant Huber. A tall, strapping man who marched the young soldiers hard. They headed out after breakfast across the mile-long parade field.

One soon discovered that keeping up with Lt. Huber required a whole day. "Man, could that white boy march!" L.E. recalled.

L.E.'s unit elected him as the Guide-On Bearer. Naturally, he had to be posted behind the "long-legged yahoo of a commander," as he called Lt. Huber. The team admired that man with a good style. Though L.E.'s declared a pleasant stay, everyone got along well enough at Camp Roberts' segregated barracks.

L.E. did witness racism at Camp Roberts, and they had segregated barracks. For example, a colored trainee named Connors always hid under his bunk after their morning marches to catch a quick nap. Another trainee from a separate barracks, Anderson, a young white boy with red hair and freckles, noticed this habit and believed him to be lazy. So he decided to have the white soldiers teach Connors a lesson.

Somehow, the word about this lesson got out. Billy Beck, a trainee, went to L.E.'s bunk that night to inform him of the plan. L.E. told Beck to alert the other colored soldiers.

When Anderson and his gang came to the barracks, he yelled, "Connors, we're gonna whup your ass!"

L.E. stood in the aisle, faced Anderson, and said, "If you want Connors, here he is. But nobody else betta lay a hand on 'em. So it will just be the two of ya slugging it out."

Anderson declared, "We don't have anything against anybody else; we just want lazy Connors."

L.E. again told him, "It will be the two of ya or all of 'em. Cuz ya got to bring ass to get ass. Ya ready for that?"

Anderson and his friends hemmed and hawed for a while, and the white crowd dispersed.

The barracks incident's a prime example of how L.E. stood in defense of the underdog. First, he defended a boy who'd gotten a bloody nose in elementary school. Then, L.E. evened up the matter by giving that bully a bloody nose. Subsequently, there were many individual scuffles in the military camp, but another group incident never occurred.

The young men would complete their basic training, get two weeks' leave, and report to Camp Stoneman in California. Then, they would prepare for the long, grueling trip overseas, with stops in Honolulu, Guam, and the Philippines. The stay in Manilla would be one month at Fort Clark Air Base.

In the Philippines, L.E. found acclimating to the environment difficult. Even the mere thought of eating made him want to throw up for a few days, but his appetite slowly returned. L.E. began by eating small amounts of the food in the mess hall, and soon his health improved.

L.E.'s army unit shipped out to Yokohama, Japan, and from there to Busan, South Korea, and by train to Yeongdeungpo, Korea. The soldiers piled up in two-and-a-half-ton trucks and rode to the 45th Engineering M&S Company for interviews and assignments. A taxing trip.

Major Somers interviewed L.E. for a typing position. However, L.E. didn't know how to type. Major Somers stated that someone with L.E.'s distinctive educational background and test results should take typing because he may become the company clerk with Sergeant First Class's rank when he returned to the States.

The major told him to go to the Second Army and enroll in the typing course. In the meantime, L.E. became a motor vehicle dispatcher, a clerical job he quickly mastered. Chief Warrant Officer Duffy and Sergeant First Class Grant ran the motor pool; L.E. thought they were lovely people with whom to work. He worked a twenty-four-hour shift and was off for forty-eight hours. L.E. planned to use his time off for typing classes.

Duffy and Grant were strict about orders, but their friendly attitudes made L.E. feel good about following their rules. He enjoyed working at the motor pool so much that he never enrolled in typing classes. L.E. didn't go to OCS because he didn't like the idea of such strict regimentation. He would eventually learn to type independently—using his two forefingers.

Sergeant First Class would be the designation upon class completion. That change in rank might have tempted L.E. to re-enlist. But unfortunately, military life wasn't for him. He despised the poor condition of their living quarters, yelling, and the regimen.

He did an exemplary job as a motor vehicle clerk, putting him on the way to becoming a sergeant until he got crossed up with a captain who thought that L.E. and he were seeing a woman named Miss Kim. Regrettably, L.E.'s non-interest didn't matter because the captain already believed otherwise. So when the time arrived, no promotion came down.

The first sergeant came to the motor pool and explained why the officers passed on L.E. for a promotion. The First Sergeant didn't know if the reason for L.E.'s denial was valid, but L.E. never confronted the captain. He merely told the sergeant that the captain barked up the wrong tree and interest in Miss Kim did not exist. Miss Kim was the least of his worries, with little time left in Korea.

One night the officers were having a party in the Bachelor Officer Quarters (B.O.Q.). Colonel Kibler, commander of the 45th Engineering, requested that Cpl. Worley go to the 8th Army Headquarters in Seoul and picks up some of his friends. Before this occasion, Col. Kibler wrote a directive that stated, "No one can take a motor vehicle out after 1800 hours without an authorized permission slip, signed by Kibler. The Colonel did so after he got wind of unauthorized vehicle usage and was determined to stop such activities.

After midnight, L.E. had to be available for late-night requests. So, he stripped down to his skivvies and got in the cot. But, no sooner did he get tucked in when a knock came at the door. And, before Bennett could say anything, in strolled Col. Kibler, a Major General, a Brigadier General, and another full Colonel.

Kibler displayed a strange smile on his face. "Hi, Corporal Bennett. I want to get my vehicle to take my friends back to the 8th Army Headquarters in Seoul. I'll also need one of your drivers."

Still in his cot, L.E. politely replied, "Yes, sir! If you sign an authorization slip, I'll have a driver take care of you."

The response from Kibler sounded as if a 105 Howitzer fired. The sound almost shattered L.E.'s eardrum.

"Get out of that cot and get my vehicle!"

L.E. jumped out of the sweet, warm spot and stood in his skivvies.

"Stand at attention, Corporal," Col. Kibler barked.

Looking directly at Col. Kibler, L.E. said, "Sir, you have a directive that states no vehicle can leave this motor pool unless you first sign an authorization."

The Colonel changed his facial expression. L.E. followed orders as trained. Then, looking at Bennett, Kibler's face reddened, and he grumbled, "Where in the Hell is the damn authorization slip?" Kibler signed it, and he went off to Seoul.

The following day at the motor pool, Officer Duffy came to see L.E., who steeled himself for another scolding, but Officer Duffy had another message. Col. Kibler had asked Duffey to commend L.E. for sticking to his guns. Because, if L.E. had the Colonel sign an authorization form, he was undoubtedly making everyone else complete a form.

"Between the two of us," Officer Duffy told L.E., "the next time Col. Kibler comes over during the night for a vehicle, give him the whole damn motor pool if he wants it, damn it."

L.E. and Duffy both laughed.

Most importantly, L.E. had a newfound respect for the Colonel. Whenever Col. Kibler wanted his vehicle after 1800 hours, he ensured a driver signed a requisition slip.

On a hot summer evening, L.E. sat outside the Dispatch Office when Private Pace visited him. Sergeant First Class (S.F.C.) Grant had asked Pace to go north to the demilitarized zone and pick up a loaned-out jeep. L.E. had never been up north, so he was excited to make the trip.

They rose early to leave the base the following day for Yeongdeungpo. Beautiful scenery, with tall green trees surrounded by lush vegetation. As Pace drove, L.E. surveyed the plants. He didn't remember any landscape upon their first arrival, and the air was so fresh. Then, finally, a part of Korea that he had not had the opportunity to see, so he sat back and enjoyed it.

They left Yeongdeungpo around noon and arrived by early evening at the demilitarized zone (D.M.Z.). The Motor Sergeant greeted Bennett and Pace, advising they make themselves at home. Thankfully, their fellowship included a few cold ones, and they decided to head back to Yeongdeungpo.

Pace drove the lead jeep with L.E. following close behind. On the mountainous terrain, they drove carefully because of the winding roads. Occasionally, L.E. would be out of Pace's view while going around a curve. As they proceeded down the mountain, L.E. hit some loose gravel and went off the road. Only part of the jeep hung on the side of the hill. Afraid to move for fear the vehicle would tumble down the mountainside, L.E. sat motionlessly. His only hope was that Pace would look back and realize he was no longer following him. Talk about living in momma's prayers.

He sat waiting for Pace, L.E. let his mind race back to Camp Roberts. At that moment, L.E. recalled when he assisted in fighting a forest fire in the San Joaquin Valley. While on a rest break from firefighting, the men decided to hike up the mountain and watch the fire. L.E.'s foot hit loose dirt at some point, and he began to slide down the side of that mountain.

L.E. grunted as he slid down and tried to break his fall. Shaking his head, he desperately tried to clear the dust from his eyes and the dirt falling in his mouth. Then, reaching out, he grabbed a sapling growing from the side of the mountain. It broke his slide.

After regaining his footing and being assisted up, L.E. looked closer at the small plant that had saved his life. It grew in loose dirt and came out effortlessly with one yank of his hand.

His life flashed before him as he thought about how his momma's prayers and God's grace had kept him from going off the side of that mountain and falling five hundred feet over jagged rocks. There was no way a little sapling could break the slide of a 6'2", 195-pound man. For L.E., it was the hand of God.

He was again on another mountain with his life in the balance. His prayer life stopped once he left home. As the minutes ticked by and Pace hadn't returned, L.E. began to pray. Soon he saw lights coming back up the mountain. It was Pace, answering L.E.'s prayers. Pace used a chain, connected it, and pulled L.E.'s jeep back to its center.

Pace and L.E. would stay within eyesight of each other back to Yeongdeungpo. They arrived late that night and spent a good deal of the next day in their bunks. L.E. would never forget Pace's friendship and heroic efforts to save his life.

First, Sergeant Savage tried to get L.E. to re-enlist, stating he was guaranteed a promotion. But L.E. sat his eyes on seeing his family again. He'd had enough of military adventures. L.E. wanted to finish his term and move on with his life.

Change

It's always hard to be the first one to go
Through and bust down the door.
It's easy to be part of a big crowd, but who will
Step forward to lead and make the dangerous,
unpopular quest for change.

Nothing will happen if you don't speak up.
Change is always a dangerous game!

Sharon Bennett 2019

L.E. graduated Magna Cum Laude, Class Valevictorian
1953

New Enlistment for the Korean War

39

 L.E. receiving award for fighting California Wildfire while at Camp Roberts

 L.E. in Korea at the Motor Pool

Army Base Picnic

 L.E. in >>> middle, Pace up front

New Hope Singers Program>>> (L-R) Back Row 1st-Floyd, 2nd-Ray, 3rd-Ruel

^(L-R) Ray, Ruel, L.E. and Ruel, Jr., Martha's spouse and child

New Hope Singers (L-R)>>> 1st-Ruel, 4th-Ray, 5th-Floyd

<<<New Hope Singers, (L-R) 4th-L.E., 5th-Floyd, 6th-Ray

6

Twinkie

In March 1954, L.E. arrived in El Campo for military leave, excited to be with his mother again. Anice looked well. They stayed up all night talking about the happenings around town.

She wanted to ask how her son liked the army. L.E. assured her that discharge in June 1956 couldn't roll around rapidly enough. Many benefits existed to military life for many, but not for him. He didn't like obeying orders as part of a mindless group. During the next few days of leave, L.E. visited old friends and allowed Anice, as she repeatedly said, to show off her tall, healthy, handsome son to friends.

All week Mount Olive Baptist, L.E.'s home church, held a revival in the schoolhouse. Pastor A.A. Hargrove hosted Rev. B.F. Langham from Mt. Calvary Baptist of San Antonio. Since L.E.'s been home, his mother attended services without him. She continued to sing in the choir with her beautiful contralto voice. Anice also directed the children's choir. L.E. discerned she would be happy for him to attend.

L.E. ignored the spiritual urge to minister for several years. Ordinarily, L.E. stayed up in the West End (Ox Blood) with the fellows. But even being Friday night, L.E. felt compelled to go.

Entering through the church vestibule, L.E. observed the building was packed. Tempted to sit up front in the family's old pew, L.E. took a seat on the left side, facing the pulpit. After a while, he noticed a young lady ushering. Essie Lee Jones, the girl he had asked for a date after her basketball games during high school. She told him to get lost.

Admiring a bright yellow aura around the girl, L.E. realized Essie had grown into a gorgeous woman. He decided to try talking to her again. After all, not seeing anyone currently, nor being the playboy anymore; maybe Essie would give him the time of day.

What did he have to lose? He watched Essie throughout the service. She didn't appear to be aware of him. Instead, she stayed busy at her ushers' posts.

L.E. patiently waited for the end of service and benediction as his mind wandered back to the many revivals he and his family attended. His brother Carl answered the call to discipleship and sat on the mourner's bench every church revival. Carl accepted Christ and got baptized every time.

The Bennett clan sat in the same pew every Sunday. Then, finally, time rolled around for the invitation to discipleship. Carl prepared to stand, and Dan swiftly grabbed him by the arm.

Speaking in a low growl, "Sit down, boy. Don't ya go up there! If ya ain't got the Holy Ghost by now, ya ain't gonna get it. Now, sit back. What ya doing anyway, that ya gotta keep going to the mourner's bench for, huh?"

Carl lowered his head and quietly slid back into his seat.

L.E. laughed to himself about the memory and quickly remembered his position, in church. Finally, benediction came, services ended, and worshippers headed outside. L.E. waited out front for Essie to emerge from the building. Then, as she appeared, he approached her.

"Hi, Essie. How are you?"

"Well, look who's here. If it isn't Mr. America."

They began a casual conversation. Essie looked forward to graduating from high school and moving. However, she remained undecided whether to attend college or move to a big city and work.

Essie tried to act casually about L.E., but she was very interested. Since his playboy days in high school, L.E. joined the army and traveled. All the things she hoped to do. Maybe he'd grown up. In front of her stood this tall, dark, and handsome man she had blown off back in high school.

L.E. asked if she was seeing anyone. He didn't keep tabs on her but heard she and Elroy Perkins were an item, one of his classmates.

"No, I'm not particularly interested in anybody at present."

L.E. tilted his head and gave his winning boyish grin. "Well, Essie, will you go out with me next Saturday night?"

Essie clasped her hands in front of her and replied, "Yes!"

She would come to town and stay with Andy Hamilton, her grandfather. L.E. could pick her up there. They bade each other goodnight as the crowd dispersed. Anice exited the church, smiling.

On the stroll home, L.E. told his mother, "I think I've just met the girl I'm going to marry."

"Oh, who?" Anice asked.

"Essie Lee Jones," replied L.E.

"Sho' 'nuff? Well, I tell ya one thing. She sure is a sweet girl and will probably make ya a good wife. But, I didn't know ya two was courting."

L.E. explained to his mother what happened and how he saw the bright aura around Essie as she stood in the choir stand. Anice chuckled and told L.E. he might have been right about his prediction.

L.E. could hardly wait for Saturday night to roll around. He put on some of his best clothes and cologne. He said, "My Right Guard and my left guard, too." He walked to an area of town called Mays Addition, where Essie awaited his arrival. He made small talk with her grandfather, step-grandmother, and uncles. Eventually, Essie stood, signaled L.E., and moved towards the door. L.E. stood and held the screen door open for Essie to exit, and he turned to say goodnight to the family.

Looking at L.E. with a sly grin, Essie's grandfather said, "Careful, she has hips like her grandmother Pearcie, and she'll have baby after baby on ya, like her grandmother."

L.E. frowned, said goodnight, and they left for the Normandy Theater.

They enjoyed the double feature, chatting, eating popcorn, and sipping soda. Afterward, L.E. walked Essie three miles back to Mays Addition. He asked if he could revisit her. She agreed to date him and promised to write once he returned to the military. Of course, L.E. remembered his manners and upbringing. He planned to meet Essie's parents, Sallie and Dave Jones. The next day, he hurriedly went to see them at their farm near El Campo. L.E. asked Mr. Jones for permission to court his daughter.

Mr. Jones not only granted his permission but also gave L.E. advice. He took the pipe out of his mouth and pointed at the young suitor.

"You are always ta bring Essie home the same way you pick her up.

Understand? Essie is good and kind-hearted, and I don't wanna have any trouble from ya, young man. I know yo momma, and I knew yo daddy. But, if anythin' was ta happen ta Essie, I' ma come lookin' fo' ya."

L.E. acknowledged the man's words. He could see they were a proud and loving family like his own. However, Essie's family history would prove to be just as impressive.

Essie's great-grandfather immigrated from Eastern Europe, South of Moscow, around 1800 and settled in upper New York. After a few years in upstate New York, the family migrated to North Carolina. Her great-grandfather, David Thornton, left home at sixteen and headed for Texas. He settled in Lavaca County, becoming a farmer. In 1884, he married Rosa Orange, a Creole from New Orleans. He came into wealth with assistance from his family and bought a farm; he's also a minister. The couple had four children. Born in 1886, Pearcie Thornton—Essie's grandmother— was the eldest.

Pearcie was a beautiful, fair-skinned, slender girl with long, thick black curly hair and light hazel eyes. Against her father's wishes, Pearcie ran off to marry a dirt-poor, dark-skinned sharecropper, Andy Hamilton, her senior by several years. David Thornton disowned Pearcie as she left the family farm on a wooden wagon with Andy. Pearcie birthed five children in succession, dying shortly after the fifth child, Sallie. Andy Hamilton brazenly had moved his mistress and her two older children into his home to assist Pearcie with her last delivery.

Pearcie's screams, yelling for help and calling for her father traumatized the elder children during the birth of her fifth child. No one called the midwife, doctor, or minister. Word of Pearcie's illness reached her family. Upon Mr. Thornton's arrival, he found Andy had commenced Pearcie's burial under a tree on a hill. Enraged, Mr. Thornton cursed Andy and returned to the train station with his associate ministers. No one found a marriage or a death record for Pearcie Thornton Hamilton. The mistress stayed with Andy in Mays Addition, raising all the children,

L.E. and Essie had a great time on dates. He repeatedly said to himself; *I'm not letting her go. I'm going to hold on to this woman.*

His leave ended in the first part of April. When L.E. returned to Texas, he and Essie were married on September 20, 1955. Reverend A.A. Hargrove, the Mt. Olive Baptist Church pastor, officiated over the ceremony at his own home. After that, L.E. and Essie moved to San Antonio, setting up housekeeping. Essie first stayed with L.E.'s sister Norcie while he returned to finish his military tour.

Next, the young couple moved in with his brother Carl and his wife, Eva, in the Wheatley Courts Apartments, on San Antonio's east side. These beautiful and affordable courts had become known as projects.

Essie was the brightest spot in L.E.'s life. She was loving, caring, and sharing—just like his mother. Essie was sweet and giving but tough, and you couldn't use her. L.E. called her Twinkie.

Their first child, Louis Ervin Bennett, was born on January 27, 1956. (L.E. named his first son.) During his birth, L.E. was at Fort Lawton, Washington. His military company's basketball team had just won their game when Norcie called from San Antonio and told him he was the father of a healthy baby boy. The following day the brand-new father called Essie, the brand-new mother, to say he loved her. He was anxious for his June 7, 1956, discharge date. When he arrived home, L.E. was overwhelmed by his new son and couldn't hold him enough.

During Essie and L.E.'s stay with Carl and Eva, L.E.'s brothers Floyd and Ray asked him to sing with the New Hope Singers. They were a male group outside of the regular choir at New Hope Baptist Church. The group received frequent requests to sing at other churches or events.

Good-looking men in a singing group attract the attention of women. Especially a lot of single women in the church. After the programs, the singers—Ray, Floyd, Ruel, A. Richardson, and L.E.—would enjoy the refreshments and chat with the guests, shaking hands and receiving hugs. Often, the women would solicit for more than conversation.

L.E. didn't have a car, so his brothers would pick him up and bring him home. Therefore, if they dilly-dallied too long, L.E. would get home late. Essie didn't appreciate it, and that led to a few disagreements. One such dispute was why L.E. had lipstick on his shirt collar. He didn't notice and couldn't explain. Eventually, he apologized and conversed with his brothers about not procrastinating anymore.

The couple had four blessed births: Louis Ervin, Sharon Kay, Kenneth Lyle, and Lisa. The boys were dark brown-skinned like their daddy, and the girls had big eyes like L.E. but were a lighter complexion like their mother.

Despite facing many challenges and crises, the couple's union was a terrific experience. L.E. found Essie to be dependable when all else was going wrong; she gave a calming voice to the situation and clearly and concisely understood.

The marriage wasn't perfect; there were as many ups as downs. Sometimes, stressors seriously threatened the continuation of their marriage. During all of L.E.'s travels, work issues, and time in school, Essie met these bumps in the road with few complaints but a lot of understanding. She would recognize that L.E. needed to spend much time away from home.

Essie made sure their room was always neat and clean. She kept their clothes clean and ironed and prepared his meals. Essie used coupons and shopped at second-hand stores like nobody's business to make it possible to be well-dressed. She was an excellent cook, as well. As a child, Essie had cooked meals for her younger siblings while her parents worked on the farm. She also stayed prepared to work a part-time job to feed their family if the employer fired him. For all these reasons and so many more, L.E. considered Essie the love of his life.

I Never Dreamed

I never knew with whom all my dreams would come true,
Now I know because God blessed me with you.
Someone to share all the seasons in time,
Someone who would only be mine,
Now I know that all the while for whom I
was waiting when I saw your smile.
You have changed my life with the warmth of
your love, and with you, I feel safe.
Now is the beginning of all we will share.
To you, I want to give myself.
Two separate souls, joined by one beautiful love—Jesus.

Sharon Bennett 2000

7

Work Begins

Discharged from the army in June 1956, it was job hunting time, and he placed applications everywhere. No offers came for L.E. and Essie with little money for a growing family. But they did allow themselves an occasional treat of a romantic night at the drive-in movies. There they carved some time alone to enjoy each other. Yet, L.E. never lost focus because he needed a job.

As the sun began to sink slowly in the west and a light breeze cooled the family, L.E. and Essie decided to visit his sister Martha on this particular summer evening. They took a pleasant stroll over to Onslow Street with baby Louis in L.E.'s arms. They sat out in the backyard swapping tall tales with his sister and Ruel, her husband.

Martha asked her brother, "How's the job hunting going?"

L.E. looked down at his bottled beer, exhaled sharply, and clicked his tongue. "I haven't found anything worthwhile yet."

"Well, have you applied at the company, Southwestern Bell?"

L.E. admitted he hadn't. He submitted requests at different local businesses for management training. At least, when the employer allowed him to do so, however, he liked the suggestion of applying to the phone company. The sibling told L.E. her neighbor worked there and gave it good marks.

So the next day, L.E. went downtown to Southwestern Bell on Travis Street. A tall building of concrete, tiled floors, and bad lighting. He went through the back door and followed the signs to the employment office, where a pale, chubby woman in her mid-fifties with short curly hair greeted L.E., named Mrs. Margaret Mitchell.

L.E. showcased his pressed navy slacks and a crisp white short-sleeved shirt. He smiled at the lady and said, "Good morning; I'm interested in applying for a job, please."

The human resource representative handed L.E. the forms while looking over the black-framed glasses that sat on her nose. She explained Southwestern Bell would happily consider him but couldn't promise anything.

Once he completed the form, she reviewed it and asked him what he would like. L.E. told her something that put him in line with management. Then, Mrs. Mitchell, with raised eyebrows, said to him that all they could offer a colored person was janitorial or garage-man work, both paying about $3 a day.

"Are you still interested?"

Silent for a few moments, L.E. considered the runaround and the menial offer. Then the twenty-three-year-old smiled at Mrs. Mitchell and declared brightly, "Yes, ma'am, I'm still interested."

Mrs. Mitchell's attitude suddenly softened, watching the change in L.E.'s upbeat demeanor. She took a deep breath and exhaled softly. "I'm sorry we don't have anything better to offer. But who knows? There may be something better later on. But, conversely, that's not a promise, you understand?"

She explained that their hiring policy also required a physical exam. Moreover, if L.E. passed, they'd talk further. "Particularly for such a clean, positive, and nice-looking young man," she exclaimed.

A few days later, L.E. went downtown to the Medical Arts Building for the examination. Within a few hours, he received another call to return to the employment office as soon as possible.

When he got there, Mrs. Mitchell smiled. He passed the tests.

"Yes, Mr. Bennett," she announced, "We have an opening for a house-serviceman at the Pershing Central Office. We are considering other candidates. You still want to proceed?"

L.E. said yes and reminded the woman he had higher aspirations. In addition, he added, "The offer is fine to start."

L.E. began his work journey as a house-serviceman, the term in those days for a janitor. However, he had no intention of staying in the position forever. He planned big things for the future. He intended to get his foot in the door and make a career and life. Anice taught her son that whatever he did, to do his best and take pride, no matter how humble the job. L.E., determined to move up, believed every role was essential.

"Do you have any relatives working with our organization?" Mrs. Mitchell asked.

L.E. responded, "No."

Mrs. Mitchell cleared her throat. "I just wondered because the company's best referrals usually come from current employees."

She instructed him to take his folder to Mr. Sid Cline at the Central Office for review.

He grinned ear to ear, took the packet, and ran out. Briefly stopping, L.E. yelled back, "Thank you, Mrs. Mitchell. Thank you very much!"

L.E. jogged over to Mr. Cline's office, interviewed, and learned the company would notify him in a few days. The waiting had him on pins and needles. He paced the floor and checked to ensure the phone was plugged in and worked. Finally, the next week, the call came: L.E. must report for work at the Pershing Central Office as Mr. Cline's house-serviceman at Southwestern Bell Telephone.

The company hired L.E. on June 21, 1956. L.E. considered himself fortunate to be part of such a reputable corporation. Whenever you told someone you worked for the telephone company, they said, "You have a nice job." Regardless, a silent horror circled about the institution. This spectacle would only bother you if you wanted more out of life. All Negroes and Mexicans could work only as janitors or mechanics. They weren't allowed to apply for more.

Alexander Graham established Bell Telephone Company in 1879. Southwestern Bell Telephone's roots are in the Missouri and Kansas Telephone Company, founded in 1882. Bell is a subsidiary of AT&T, Inc., and was considered the first rung on their corporate ladder. Therefore, it is a prime target in the battle for integration. (Southwestern Bell History, Wikipedia, March 2019)

As their company name indicated, Southwestern Bell area was comprised of Texas, Okalahoma, Kansas. Arkansas, Missouri, and parts of Illonois. Mr. John Murphy, a district manager, and Mr. Cline's second-level manager; were both over W.W. Schultz, the first-line supervisor. They were all cordial men and eager to acclimate L.E. to the job.

A tall figure, Schultz, blondish-haired man, displayed a grin stretched from ear to ear. He would always greet you with a robust handshake. After explaining the job to L.E., Schultz introduced Polk, Phillip, and Martin, who would show L.E. the ropes.

Martin had a tremendous sense of humor. He would sit and tell one story after another during work breaks. They laughed until they almost cried at a tale of Martin going too fast on a back-country road.

A cop pulled Martin over, asked him to get out of the car, and said, "Look, boy, I clocked you speeding. You were doing fifty-five in a thirty-five-mile-per-hour zone."

Martin said, "I never saw a speed limit sign, and I don't believe I was speeding."

The police officer said, "Well, I'm not going to argue with you about it. If you don't think you were, you can tell the judge. So follow me, and we'll go to see the judge."

Martin followed the officer to a stately mansion, sitting way back out in the countryside on a beautiful green rolling lawn. The living room was arranged with a judge's bench and seating. The policeman told him to have a seat, and the judge would be out.

Soon, the officer came out—with a judge's robe on. He sat behind the bench and banged the gavel. "Who comes before the court?"

Martin said, "I do, your honor! How much do I owe you?"

The whole group laughed especially hard at this story. Therefore, it would not be long before L.E. developed a pet name for Martin. He started calling him "The Ole Pro," after a cartoon character used in the old Falstaff Beer commercials. Martin liked the nickname and used it proudly himself.

The employees' relationship with their supervisor was positive. Occasionally Schultz took them out for annual employee celebrations. They'd gone out to celebrate Melvin Porter's work anniversary on one occasion. They each ordered steak with jalapeno peppers. L.E., like his mother, loved spicy foods, so he had a ball with those peppers. Unfortunately, he developed an upset stomach and didn't get much sleep. He survived and was no worse for wear the following day. However, that habit would make matters for his stomach terrible.

Mr. U.S.G. Cyphers, Local #6131 union president, approached L.E. concerning joining the Communication Workers of America (C.W.A.) shortly after his employment began. He learned that L.E.'s a member of the NAACP and wanted better career opportunities for people of color, beyond positions as janitors, female office cleaners, or mechanics.

Mr. Cyphers invited him to become a member of Bell's local union. L.E. became active and attended all meetings. After his teenage experience at that restaurant in Houston, he joined the NAACP. And L.E. talked with everyone he crossed about registering to vote.

L.E. eventually became close with fellow union member Ulysses A. Axiel, whose views and actions made an indelible impression. Axiel, with a commanding personality, became one of L.E.'s most endearing friends. He periodically offered L.E. a ride to work. In addition, Axiel, a chain smoker, had a cigar or a cigarette in his mouth when he arrived at L.E.'s home in the morning. L.E. picked up smoking while in the army but stopped cold turkey for the household's health. But he was now offering a cigarette in the mornings—so L.E. accepted.

One night on the way home from work, Axiel asked, "L.E., I have a little snort under the seat. You want a sip?"

They both took a swig of alcohol. Then Axiel took a pack of cigarettes out of his front coat pocket and offered L.E. one. L.E. accepted, lit up, and began puffing.

Axiel told his passenger, "Man, if ya gonna smoke, you need to learn how to keep buying your own."

L.E. promptly reminded his new friend that he was the one who offered him the smoke in the first place. They had a massive laugh about it—typical of their fun times.

Peaceful Revolution

"Those who make peaceful revolution impossible,
make violent revolution inevitable!"
John F. Kennedy

Remarks from the first anniversary of the
Alliance for Progress, 13 March 1962

8

A Place Of Their Own

The year 1956 was full of events, both happy and sad. Louis, his firstborn in January, was par excellence. L.E. was discharged from the army that summer, finding employment shortly after. However, on December 1st, two assailants murdered his brother, Lloyd, in a low-down San Antonio café. He was shot in the head and abdomen by two assailants while arguing with his girlfriend about going home.

The medical examiner signed the death certificate on December 4th, L.E's birthday. Dealing with emotional trauma from thirty-year-old Lloyd's death was challenging for L.E. 1957 quickly approached, and another child was on the way. There was no time left for self-reflection. L.E. and Essie were hoping for a girl this time. They wanted to have four children, two of each sex. On May 3rd, a girl was born at Hicks Lying-In Hospital on South Hackberry Street in San Antonio.

L.E. named her Sharon Kay after Sharon Kay Ritchie, Miss Texas, from the 1956 Miss America competition. For the proud father, Sharon was a beautiful, fat, gray-eyed baby with big dimples on her cheeks, and she had a smile that warmed her daddy's heart. The Bennetts now had two healthy children. Louis had grown to resemble L.E. as a young'un. Sharon possessed her father's smarts and temperament but had her mother's tenderness.

One month after Sharon's birth, L.E. started the summer session at St. Phillips Junior College. He desired to further his education and found a place to rent for his growing family. He and Essie moved from his brother

Carl's to a duplex on Blaine Street, just off New Braunfels on the east side of town. Charles and Mercie Pitts lived on the duplex's other side, a young couple with children, and these two young families shared a bathroom and became friends and good neighbors.

The house was small and rundown but cheap—and full of roaches. It needed some serious elbow grease. Their family got to work with assignments from Essie on what to clean in the home. First, they swept and mopped the floors. Then, they wiped and scrubbed the walls, cabinets, tub, and toilet using Clorox. Everyone made her kitchen sparkle. Finally, L.E. and his wife applied insect spray on every inch of the house and left the home for a couple of hours, returning and going to bed.

Essie had become a member at Mt. Calvary Baptist Church of San Antonio before L.E. got discharged from the army, so he joined. It was on Poinsettia Street on the east side. The Mt. Olive Church's visiting revivalist, Langham, was one hundred miles east. Before moving to a small rental house on Yucca, the Bennett family lived in the duplex for a short while.

In 1957, L.E.'s mother, Anice, left her home in El Campo and came to live with her son and daughter-in-law until she could find her place. Anice became a tremendous help to Essie with the children. The young couple only had a two-bedroom house, but Anice was happy to sleep with her grandchildren.

Anice joined the Mt. Calvary family, too. She loved being around the children and helping to care for them. However, when Essie and L.E. went out for an evening, she gave the children candy when their mother told her not to.

Time moved fast. The kids were growing like weeds, and L.E. became more involved in union meetings and NAACP voter registration drives and kept pace with school. These were difficult times for L.E., working eight hours a day and going to school three nights a week. He got up each morning around 5 a.m. to catch a bus to work, where he was to report at 7 a.m.

L.E. preferred to arrive early, 6-6:30 a.m. if he could. He got off work at 3 p.m. and took public transportation to St. Philips Junior College. He caught the last bus home when the class ended around 9:30 p.m. L.E. would return home around 11:30 p.m. Whenever Axiel gave him a ride to and from work, it helped make for a better day. L.E. could sleep for about four hours before starting the cycle again.

In the hot, sweltering summer of 1958, L.E. enrolled again in night school at St. Philips. This time, he was in pursuit of completing his business associate degree. One day, a white co-worker saw L.E. reading during his lunch break and asked if he attended classes on the company tuition plan and the G.I. bill. L.E. stopped chewing his sandwich and looked at the man with bewilderment. Finally, L.E. responded that he knew nothing about such programs.

The craft-level employee smiled and told him that the military usually told all discharging soldiers about the G.I. bill and to check on the tuition plan forms with his supervisor. L.E. did just that. Schultz had no problem providing L.E. with what he needed. Soon enough, L.E. received financial assistance, which proved to help their household budget greatly.

For I Am

I'm here to find out if you want me,
but I'm just so hard to keep.
I bring pleasure to those who do have me,
but when I'm lost, thus the sky does weep.

I' I the joyful smile of children,
I'm the thoughts of lovers embraced,
and in the peace you find within yourself,
when you put aside your life's mistakes.

I'm sought after through all the ages,
In every culture the world around,
And died many deaths in the darkness of life,
but in this light again, I can be found.

Oh, I'm wanted for so many reasons,
some good, some bad, you would deem.
For I am what is called "Happiness."
desired by all; yes, by all indeed.

Sharon Bennett 2001

L.E. and Essie 1955 after the wedding.
And in Photo Booth 1970s

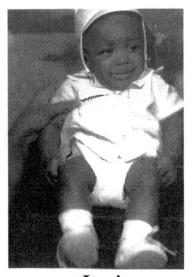

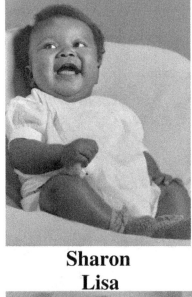

Louis
Kenneth

Sharon
Lisa

<Anice holding
Sharon, 1957

^L.E. Holding
Louis 1956

^Essie and L.E.
with Louis, 1956

^Essie with
Louis and
Sharon

Essie, L.E., and Bennett children. Baby Lisa below

Family at Playland Park

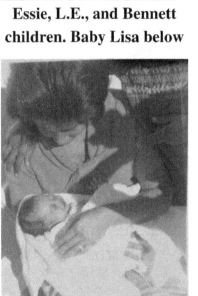

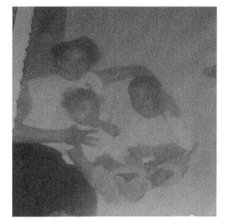

Bennett's and children

**The Family on Monterey St.,
San Antonio**

**Anice with Louis and Sharon
at relatives @1958**

Anice ^ >
<Floyd

L.E. and Ray

<<<<Ray and Doris'
Wedding (center)

Bennett's evenings out.
Above (L-R) Essie, Earline,
Floyd, L.E.

L.E. and Essie

Above Norcie on Right
Below (L-R) Mack, Ruby, Floyd's
wife, Janie Winters Bennett

Mack
and
Ruby
wedding

9

Ask What You Can Do

In the 1950s and 1960s, war raged in America: the fight against segregation, racism, and inequality. Although the battle was taken up mainly by African Americans, many people took the challenge and stood—not to allow hatred and injustice to continue.

On September 12, 1960, L.E. became impassioned as he listened to J.F.K speak in front of the Alamo in San Antonio. J.F.K and Lyndon B. Johnson (L.B.J.) had stopped in Texas during their cross-country campaign for the presidency.

Transitioning fully to the mainstream workforce would continue to confront African Americans long after slavery. As a result, equality became a hollow promise that didn't exist. Many blacks sought better lives by migrating from the South to the North during The Great Migration of 1916-1930 (Cassedy Summer 1997, Vol. 29, No. 2).

Asa Philip Randolph of New York was a prominent civil rights movement leader in the American labor movement and socialist political parties. In 1925, he organized and led the Brotherhood of Sleeping Car Porters (B.S.C.P.), the first predominantly African American labor union. In the early civil rights and labor movements, Randolph was an unsilenced voice; his continuous agitation against unfair labor practices concerning people of color came with the support of fellow labor rights activists.

Eventually, his protests led President Franklin D. Roosevelt to issue Executive Order 8802 in 1941, which banned discrimination in the defense industries. The group then successfully pressured President Harry

S. Truman to release Executive Order 9981 in 1948, ending segregation in the armed services and regarding hiring by unions and employers (Wikipedia. org, A. Philip Randolph, n.d.).

Back in 1941, A. Philip Randolph announced the creation of a March on Washington Committee, promising that unless President Roosevelt issued the executive order, 10,000 Americans would march through Washington, D.C., to demand an end to segregation. Randolph threatened that the number of marchers would grow if ignored.

Tallies went from 10,000 to 50,000, and then to 100,000. Eventually, despite the pleas of Roosevelt and his intermediaries, Randolph made it clear nothing less than a presidential executive order would stop the march. Roosevelt gave in and issued Executive Order 8802 (Wikipedia. org, A. Phillip Randolph, n.d.).

Roosevelt only gave in to pressure, and a prime example of his racism showed. Because after Jesse Owens won four Olympic gold medals for America against Germany in track and field in 1936 and returned home, Roosevelt wouldn't even invite the man to the White House to shake his hand.

After World War II, black labor unionism became part of a more extensive campaign for civil rights. However, after the 1955 merger of the Congress for Industrial Organization (C.I.O.) and the American Federation of Labor (A.F.L.), the result was a conservative pall (originated from the A.F.L.) over the entire organization, dividing white and black unionists (Black Workers Remember, Jacqueline Jones, 2000).

It was also the civil rights movement era—black union officials such as Ed Nixon, Roy Wilkins of the NAACP, and A. Philip Randolph were the leaders during the Montgomery bus boycott and the 1963 March on Washington. African Americans would continue to press their demands for justice in the 1960s and 1970s through internal union organizations (Black Workers Remember, Jacqueline Jones, November 30, 2000).

These unfair and oppressive conditions caused a more profound awakening in a man named L.E. Bennett from San Antonio. After being recently honorably discharged from the army in 1956, twenty-three-year-old L.E. found work as a janitor with Southwestern Bell Telephone Company. Yet, in a day's work, co-workers ignored L.E. Employees walked directly over his freshly mopped floors and never excused themselves or greeted him.

L.E. consistently monitored the company job board for four years, looking for something better but had to wait until he had been in his current position for six months and had shown a good work ethic. Finally, after six months, he went to human resources to discuss higher-paying options. But Mrs. Mitchell said he couldn't apply for another job—

nor have a position above janitorial or mechanic because he was a black man.

Outwardly, L.E. took in this situation calmly but accompanied by inner outrage. Yes, a man of color, but also an American. And he felt entitled to all the bounty this country and its job market had to offer. So, L.E. decided he could no longer go along to get along. L.E. determined his job rights extended beyond the limitations imposed illegally by white Americans. L.E. believed he was entitled to all he could earn—and he wanted it all! First, however, he realized he must have a plan.

L.E. deemed he'd be ashamed to die if he hadn't changed lives before leaving this world. The empowering words of M.L.K. and others inspired him. Their calls for justice confirmed his life's path.

During this turbulent time, twenty-seven-year-old L.E. finally chose a treacherous but decisive battle: to forge integration at Southwestern Bell/AT&T company by lobbying people of color to be eligible for positions other than lowly posts, such as janitors, mechanics, and office cleaners.

Word of the civil rights movement in Mississippi and Alabama existed everywhere. But, L.E. knew the campaign would need to cause a chain reaction across the South. Its most famous leaders were M.L.K., J.F.K., Rev. Johns, Medgar Evers, and Malcolm X. But they weren't doing it alone. They inspired many others to join them in attaining the historic step of equality for people of color. So, as they worked in the areas where they lived, L.E. would work where he lived.

Not having one possible leader, many were strength of the black community. With a murdered leader, the fight continued. Instead of quieting those many voices, they got louder. That's something racists didn't understand. There's nothing intrinsically virtuous or pragmatic about a movement with only one leader. Many unsung men and women could take up the cause and lead a change campaign.

These people—foot soldiers perhaps—are heroes, and L.E. Bennett was one of them. A courageous individual who made a good change in many lives when it was not a popular thing to do.

J.F.K.'s blondish-brown hair glistened in the sunlight, and his face appeared red from exposure. September 12, 1960, the temperature was in the 80s, and people in the audience were standing shoulder-to-shoulder with no room for air to rush through. Many had sweat running down their faces. Their clothing clung to their backs and legs.

Many folks in the audience gathered in front of the legendary Alamo in San Antonio, carrying bag lunches and thermoses of their preferred drinks as protection against the sultry weather. Brimming with the audacity of hope, these people started arriving early in the morning to hear the young senator from the East Coast, J.F.K., who was running for president, make his afternoon speech.

The merchants in the area hoped to do much business on what people promised would be a historic day. However, the large crowds waiting for J.F.K. blocked their doors from entry. In addition, they needed to make up for money lost during the lunch counter sit-ins in March by young activists. The NAACP had threatened several merchants downtown on Houston and Commerce streets with non-violent protests. Joske's, Kress, Woolworth, Greens, and L.E.'s previous employer, Sommers Drug Store.

These protests were primarily peaceful and considered a success. But when media attention wasn't present, the students and their NAACP adult leader reported being pushed, and a patron slapped one young lady. Finally, the merchants said they didn't want the continued headaches and relented.

According to L.E., Jackie Robinson, a professional baseball player, was visiting San Antonio and commented about the non-violent protests while speaking at the La Villita district.

He said, "This is a story that should be told around the world."

A New York paper quoted him the following day, Sunday, March 20, 1960; however, even though the merchants publicly agreed, they used stall tactics, had restricted hours for people of color, or flatly refused. Less violent, yes. But young people were brutally attacked, tortured, and murdered across Texas and other states during these lunch counter protests. Though a step in progress and tooted as a move that ended segregation in San Antonio, it did not.

Well, those retailers hoped for increased sales to recover from the prior demonstrations with Presidential candidate Kennedy's visit. Instead, people lined the streets and sidewalks with no room to spare, blocking entrances. L.E. Bennett was among those near the crowd, waiting to be impressed. But instead, the word was that this young senator's stunning speeches usually included talk of all races working together for a better community and a better America.

Although he had served time in the military and received a high-school diploma which was more than most management in those days, a janitorial position was the best he could hope for because of his skin color. However, L.E. had a burning desire to achieve so much more. He wanted to continue his education at a four-year university—to provide for his family and make his mother proud.

The young senator took his place with the East Coast accent and explained what he could do for our country. The young man had a charisma that caused people to like him and follow him—his way of speaking generated sincerity and hope. The San Antonio crowd listened, mesmerized.

L.E. was equally transfixed. Standing with arms crossed, listening to convincing rhetoric on the importance of sincerity, hard work, judgment on your character, not your skin color, and reaching our dreams if we all worked together.

When JFK finished his speech, the crowd erupted in thunderous applause. L.E. joined them in clapping as the image of boundless opportunities for people of color flashed before his eyes; and for the first time he felt he could do something about it. Finally, after many years of experiencing injustices based on his skin color, he dared to hope for more. Companies doing business in this city needed assimilation.

That white man, running for president of the United States, talked about creating a country where everyone can seek opportunity and realize their dreams. L.E. was enthralled. He wished to become part of that process. J.F.K. and M.L.K. would catalyze L.E.'s ideas.

It was essential to understand the Communication Workers of America's (C.W.A) history and its part with the Bell Telephone Systems/AT&T. Unionization of the telephone industry during the first thirty years of this century was a few scattered pockets of organized workers.

The first attempt was the International Brotherhood of Electrical Workers (I.B.E.W.), which accepted white women operators in 1912. However, worried about large-scale unionism, the telephone company encouraged employees to form and join company-dominated unions, which virtually destroyed the I.B.E.W. until 1935 (C.W.A.- union. Org C.W.A.-history).

Congress passed the National Labor Relations Act (Wagner Act), declaring company unions illegal. So, after years of strikes, back and forth with changes, the C.W.A. was founded in 1938 during labor meetings in Chicago and New Orleans. (It was initially known as the National Federation of Telephone Workers, becoming the C.W.A. in 1947.) At first, it stood for just the telephone industry. Today, it represents all communication areas, including healthcare, public service, and customer service (C.W.A.- union. Org C.W.A.-history).

All that the C.W.A. was fighting for didn't involve its non-white employees. Negotiations didn't include the janitors, office cleaners, and mechanics that kept their offices clean and the vehicles running. Only those who held craft positions of trained employees were of value. Furthermore, the C.W.A. collected dues from the Colored People's Unions wherever they existed. Well, L.E. Bennett would be the one to lead that change.

The Greatness to Bend History

Few will have the greatness to bend history itself, but each of us can change a small portion of events, and somebody will write the total of these acts and the history of this generation. It is from numberless diverse acts of courage and belief that human history is shaped,

Each time a man stands up for an ideal act to improve a lot of others or strikes out against injustice, he sends forth a tiny ripple of hope. And crossing each other from a million different centers of energy and daring, these ripples build a current that can sweep down the mightiest walls of oppression and resistance.

Robert Kennedy
Cape Town, South Africa
June 6, 1966

10

Time To Step Up

The children appeared near death on a hot late summer day. But, then, no definite rules existed about securing grownup business things out of prying eyes. Those days, you did as told and didn't question your parents.

Meanwhile, at work, L.E. received an annual merit increase. So now, the couple could buy a house, and on the bus route, pregnant with their third child, a car of their own became an essential detail.

L.E. called his brother Floyd to give them a ride to 1314 Ervin Street to meet Dr. Ruth Bellinger, the owner. Once Dr. Bellinger arrived, she and L.E. recognized each other from NAACP meetings. L.E. introduced Essie to Dr. Bellinger. The ladies hugged, and Ruth told them about the house and the neighborhood.

Initially, Fort Sam Houston Army Base built the neighborhood outside their south gate for housing to accommodate their non-commissioned soldiers, but it fell through. So instead, the government sold the homes to people of color. It was a small white house with a walkway from the road up to the steps. The dwelling consisted of a living area, two bedrooms, and one bathroom. Though the home didn't have a garage, it included plenty of yard space to park a vehicle off the street; it boasted a fenced backyard. Everyone loved the house. Not fancy, but clean, tidy, and a step forward for Essie and L.E.

L.E. and Essie told Ms. Bellinger they desired to take the property. The price tag came to a monthly rent of $60. It would be a lease to purchase, with a portion going toward their down payment.

Once L.E. made the initial payment amount in full, the deed closing would occur for the Bennetts. Excited about the prospect of homeownership, they hardly could contain themselves. L.E. borrowed the funds from the company credit union, and the family soon moved in. Blissful in her own tiny home. A home that didn't share walls or a bathroom.

A couple of years later, they dressed the children and took a professional photo on the couch.

Some of the most pleasant family memories about Ervin Street were when grandmother Anice came over, especially after services on Sundays. Any time spent with Anice was happy for the family. The kids loved the attention and hugs she gave them.

As they sat in the backyard and watched Louis and Sharon play, L.E. told her his hopes and dreams. He wanted to advance in his job, but minorities weren't allowed to bid for entry-level craft jobs. So as a person of color, you ended up stuck in garage-man or house-servicemen and house-servicewomen positions. He continually brought up the subject in union meetings, but they did nothing. Mr. Cyphers was a good man but ineffective and content with the little bit the employer extended.

L.E. repetitively told his fellow union members, "How can a man stand up straight if he doesn't do right?"

All the NAACP meetings L.E. attended stoked his fire; a young man full of hope, vision, promise, and integrity, and the current company union leaders weren't willing to press the issue of better career chances for minorities. Instead, the union went along with the status quo, not rocking the boat. Possibly they were afraid.

L.E. started thinking about running for president of the Communications Workers of America, local union #6131, which was for colored employees—the counterpart to the C.W.A.'s white union members at Southwestern Bell.

When L.E. revealed running for president to his mother, Anice voiced her concern about having too much on his plate. Regardless, he recognized that someone had to take a stand. Furthermore, since L.E. made it his habit to support the underdog, maybe that person needed to strengthen his union.

On August 13, 1959, around 11 p.m., Essie began to have birthing pangs. L.E. quickly took her to Robert B. Green Hospital. At approximately

1 o'clock the following day, the Bennetts had a beautiful bouncing baby boy with a head full of black curls that he would keep his whole life.

The nurse on duty was Earline, the first wife of L.E.'s brother Floyd. She went to the waiting room and asked L.E. if he wanted to see his baby boy.

Earline added, "I think we may have gotten the babies mixed up somehow because this little boy looks too much like a Mexican baby."

"What craziness are you talkin' 'bout?" L.E. asked.

The proud papa starred at his son, a caramel African-American baby with curly black hair just as cute as a button. L.E. named his third child Kenneth Lyle Bennett because his sister Norcie had asked to name him after her favorite soap opera character. Anice saw the baby and nicknamed him "Dumas" because of a local T.V. commercial from Dumas Milner Chevrolet since its animated character resembled the newborn.

Thrilled about his new son, conversely, Essie expressed a concern. Recently, Louis and Sharon had begun acting out. They were throwing tantrums and ignoring their mother's instructions to behave. How would they behave with a new brother who would dominate their mother's attention? Kenneth's arrival meant three kids under age five in the Bennett household.

In the summer of 1960, after hundreds of grueling hours of fitting in studying at St. Philips Junior College, L.E. graduated with honors with an Associate's degree in Business Administration. L.E. deemed graduation day a superb experience for him—the first and only member of his family to graduate high school and now junior college. But, of course, those were lofty goals for basic folks from the country. Essie attended the ceremony, but not Anice; she couldn't participate due to her health failing.

Dr. S.H. James, the pastor of the Second Baptist Church, preached at the graduation ceremony, "Test All Things, and Prove What is Good," from Romans 12:2. A special message to L.E. His impression was as if the preacher spoke right to him.

As the graduating class left Second Baptist Church, L.E. held his head high. College graduation was quite an accomplishment. It could mean more income and a better future for him and his family.

L.E. enrolled at St. Mary's University for September 1960 classes. He set his sights on earning a Bachelors's in Business Administration and

Marketing. His first meeting at St. Mary's was with Brother George B. Kohennon, Dean of the School of Business. Kohennon, a middle-aged man with graying hair, wore horn-rimmed glasses. After cordial introductions and handshakes, he directed L.E. to take a seat.

Dean Kohennon inquired, "L.E., why do you want to be a marketing major in business?"

"I want to be a top-flight manager with some successful company," L.E. replied, "and hopefully, someday own a successful business. Something that belonged to me."

"Well, I think that is admirable on your part to have such high expectations, but I think you need to be realistic," Kohennon responded. "There doesn't seem to be a desire to hire Negro managers. So you will probably have to seek employment in some of the northern states or stick with the Negro professions—such as medicine, law, or school teaching for other Negroes."

"I desire to be a manager," L.E. reiterated. "Not a lawyer, doctor, nor school teacher. I don't see why I should have to go up north to find a job when there must be jobs available right here."

The Dean reassured L.E. that St. Mary's University had an excellent School of Business, but he needed to explain the situation candidly. L.E. thanked him for his honesty.

At this time, L.E.'s life had become disorganized and tumultuous, given union responsibilities on top of the school work. As a result, L.E. stretched in many directions. Nonetheless, he was excited about being at St. Mary's University. It's a historical Catholic college, and most instructors were priests or nuns. Nevertheless, L.E. found the instructors cordial, helpful but demanding—just as they should be. He never experienced any direct negative attitude from classmates or instructors—only the occasional side glance in the hallway as he walked past proudly.

One chilly fall evening, L.E. attended his first marketing class. The instructor was Mr. William Peery, a slender gentleman with substantial gray hair who spoke with a lisp. A horseback riding enthusiast, he often arrived to class in his riding garb: a gray Stetson set somewhat to the left side of his head, jacket with matching pants, spit-shined boots, and crop.

On the first night of class, Mr. Peery warned students that he would not give students any A's. Instead, Peery said the author was the "A," and he's the "B." After that, the class knew they were in for a rough ride. Peery turned out to be tough but fair at times.

L.E.'s classwork competed with his union work and NAACP duties—and sometimes suffered.

Meanwhile, L.E. relocated to the central offices. The telephone company moved employees around so that an employee wouldn't be a stranger to that office when someone went on vacation. As the low person in seniority, L.E. had to take those new assignments. The downside was working some Sundays, which kept him from attending church with his family.

The most challenging assignment entailed working out at Lackland Air Force Base because of the distance from home. People at the facility were always cordial. Nevertheless, it made it difficult for L.E. to complete the trip and return to his union and school duties without transportation. It required a lot of advanced arrangements and connections. It conclusively occurred to L.E. that he needed a car. He couldn't keep borrowing his brothers' cars for out-of-town union or family business.

L.E. received an annual merit increase; from that, he and Essie had saved for a house. However, his priority now was buying a car. So, during his break time, he scanned through the newspaper and located a used car lot on West Commerce Street. Also, he planned to visit one day on his transit route. Alas, the day he chose, it rained heavily. But two young salesmen were eager to sell L.E. a car.

He selected a black 1951 Chevy four-door sedan. L.E. got permission to take a test drive. He attempted to start the engine, but it wouldn't turn over. One salesman assessed the situation and determined that the car needed a jump-start. He retrieved a battery charger and hooked the cables. That time the motor turned over.

L.E. took the car for a drive. It ran well, so he was ready to negotiate a price. L.E. accepted the necessary papers that he and Essie must review and sign later. He exited the little tin hut, got into the vehicle, turned the key, and again, it wouldn't start.

The salesman grabbed the cables and applied the juice again. Eventually, the car roared to life, and L.E. was off and running.

However, as he drove downtown and stopped at a red light, the engine died. He hit the starter, but the motor wouldn't turn over. L.E. covered his face with his hands and groaned. He was exhausted from school, work, and union activities. Plus, he desperately needed a car.

He took the key from the ignition and placed it under the front floor mat. Then, he put his hat on, buttoned up his coat, grabbed his duffle bag, locked the doors, and departed to a payphone to call the dealer to explain what had happened.

The salesperson offered to come out and give the Chevy another jump. But L.E. had had enough. He explained where he parked the car and where the salesman could find the keys. L.E. then got off the phone, anchored his hat, grabbed his brown briefcase and coat collar, and ran for the bus stop. One block up, the wind was howling in his ears, and the rain intensified, but L.E. made it just in time to catch the last bus home.

It was a dry, sunny fall day, and Essie worked her garden outside. She was born and bred in the country, she had many skills, and gardening was her forte. She could grow fresh fruits and vegetables with her eyes closed, but flowers and decorative plants were her passion. Essie loved math and was an excellent student also.

Essie's other chore was to tear apart an old baby mattress to make pillows with the filling. But, of course, when every penny counted, you didn't throw away anything that could serve another purpose.

All three of the children were playing in the fenced backyard near her. However, that old mattress with coils became a tyrant, and Essie was determined not to allow defeat. Regrettably, young parents weren't mindful of the quietness of children as a warning sign.

Sharon went back into the house, and Kenneth followed her. Sharon climbed onto the toilet, scaled along the tub's rim, and jumped into the sink, opening the medicine cabinet and getting a big bottle of pills with a loose top. She handed the bottle to her little brother and then hung-dropped to the floor from the sink.

"Mom, can I have some candy, too?" Louis whined as he ran up to Essie.

Stopping what she was doing, Essie annoyingly asked Louis, "What candy, boy," surveying the yard for Sharon and Kenneth while Louis answered.

The five-year-old pointed back to the house, "They have candy and won't give me any."

Essie gasped as she dropped everything, running into the house and seeing her two youngest children sprawled on the bathroom floor. The white aspirin tablets from the large glass bottle were scattered about and dried residue was on the childrens' mouths.

Kenneth, twenty-four months old, and Sharon, a four-year-old, were chewing the aspirin, as their stained faces displayed the marks from the pills mixed with their saliva.

"No. No. Oh, my God."

Essie frantically ran to her bedroom to grab her keys and threw her purse over her shoulder. She snatched Kenneth and Sharon under each arm like a couple of potato sacks and beckoned for Louis to follow her. Then, throwing them into the car's back seat, L.E.'s brother Floyd had loaned them. She told Louis to hold onto them. Sharon and Kenneth had fallen asleep.

Essie had never been on the highway before, but she had driven a tractor in the fields. Moreover, she had been to the stores in her vicinity. Essie turned the car on, screeched back out of the driveway, and stepped on the gas, tearing down the street. She didn't have time to wash up dirty clothes and hair strewn.

The family arrived at the Robert B. Green Emergency Room on Fort Sam Houston Army Base within minutes. As Essie slammed the brakes, the car tires shrieked in front of the main entrance. She hastened out of the car, gathered the kids, and ran inside. Louis closely followed her every step.

Essie yelled desperately, "Help me. Please, help. My kids ate a lot of aspirin."

The nuns ran over to her, snatched the two children, and rushed them into a procedure room. The doctor ran in, and they were in a frenzy working on the kids, quickly placing I.V.s for fluids and pumping their stomachs.

While Essie and Louis waited for an update, she called L.E. to apprise him of their situation. Instead of going home, he took the bus to check on his family. L.E. jumped off in front of the medical facility and headed to the entrance.

The clerk told him that they had already gone up to their room. He was so flustered when he entered the pediatric ward. He kissed the sleeping kids and turned to Essie, sitting in a rocking chair between the two beds.

He kissed her and asked how she was doing. L.E. extended his hands to assist her up to hug and console her.

L.E. smiled and asked, "So, how's our resident cat and her little brother?"

"They'll be fine. I prayed about it. Sharon's in diapers because she's pooping a lot."

Unfortunately, the IV wouldn't stay in Kenneth's small arms. The doctor cautioned Essie that Kenneth's condition was dangerous due to the amount of medication compared to his size. Nevertheless, Essie stayed up, spoon-feeding him water throughout the night. Louis lay asleep on a rollout bed that the nurse had provided. L.E. awakened Louis and took him to his mother, Anice. A few days later, the hospital released the children home.

That Saturday, L.E. went downtown to Bexar Motors and purchased a 1951 gray Dodge four-door. He and Essie would drive it until times got better financially and trade up. Then, no matter the emergency, they would have a car available.

Be Patient

All is not what it seems.
The world may seem so mean.
Give things time. Have patience and wait. When the time
is right, things will be straight. Don't rush God.
Don't rush fate.
Just be patient, and wait!

Sharon Bennett 2001

11

What Now, Mr. President?

L.E. loved being a union member because he experienced part of something important—an organization that affected change for its people. He participated in every meeting, asking questions, or making suggestions. His concerns focused on ways to advance positions for Negros within the company. Well dressed, well-read, friendly, and a perfectionist; L.E. also had a significant presence. A fire formed within him; others saw. These qualities would convince colleagues to nominate him for president of C.W.A. Local #6131.

Nominations for L.E. came when J.F.K. ran for president of the United States. Civil rights came off the back burner and finally received a prominent place in Americans' minds. Asa Randolph; M.L.K., Whitney Young; James Farmer; Thurgood Marshall; Roy Wilkins, national president of the NAACP; among others, challenged the status quo and drew newspaper headlines.

Far as L.E. was concerned, J.F.K. was also saying everything right. L.E. never forgot seeing him up close with L.B.J. at the Alamo on such a memorable day. He recalled the redness of J.F.K.'s face from exposure to the Sun. His speech was awe-inspiring. The presidential campaign visit came at a pivotal time for L.E. Southwestern Bell had hired him in late 1956; he had been a dutiful employee and an NAACP member assisting in registering voters. He was now running for president of the people of color's union.

J.F.K's speech only deepened the conviction in L.E.'s heart. He had the drive to be a force in this process of change. So L.E. departed the gathering in San Antonio and headed home with a renewed determination to do something for the colored employees at Southwestern Bell.

He wouldn't be a token leader. If elected, L.E. would focus on making things better for his colleagues and their families. L.E. had a vision: He was motivated to lobby for equal rights at Southwestern Bell and the other AT&T companies in Texas. Working against a deeply ingrained legacy of inequity wouldn't be an easy task. White people hadn't had to compete for their positions, even without education. Instead, they got a job because they were acquainted or their skin color.

L.E. was a committed supporter of the Democratic Party—and would stay so for the rest of his life. He no longer immersed himself in wishful thinking but instead moved to achieve his dreams.

J.F.K. had no personal awareness of this man whose life he had affected, but L.E. had changed nonetheless. It was time for the torch to be passed from the union's old guard to a younger generation with a bold vision for the future. Empty promises must be a thing of the past; he could accept only concrete results.

Like J.F.K., M.L.K. was a handsome fellow with polished speeches that captivated audiences. L.E. never witnessed M.L.K. in person—only on T.V. The tremendous speaker made him feel good to be of color. M.L.K. spoke with forcefulness that reached out and grabbed L.E. by the throat, inspiring him to enter into the fray to obtain an opportunity for all.

After one listened to M.L.K. speak, it's as though he was deliberating some matter of crucial importance. His concern seemed wrapped up in men and women's struggle, denied freedom of opportunity for centuries, not in the present moment. It's as if he heard unborn generations crying; they no longer would be rejected.

The expression in his voice bared the pain of W.E.B Du Bois, Booker T. Washington, Sojourner Truth, Harriet Tubman, and Frederick Douglass—pioneers who had previously articulated the things M.L.K. vocalized. During his later "I Have a Dream" speech at the Washington Monument, it was as if M.L.K. spoke personally to L.E., reminding him of his desires.

Beckoned by two men he admired, it was as if J.F.K. had given L.E. the candle, but M.L.K. had furnished the fuel for ignition. Those two men lit a fire deep in L.E.'s soul, and it now burned bright. Pushing would be a risk at this period, but a chance L.E. had to take. His new path in life was apparent. People needed better jobs than they currently had, and God had gifted L.E. with the talent to accomplish the task.

In late fall 1960, he began an intense campaign for union president. First, L.E. called members to introduce himself. Then, he passed out flyers, shook hands, and promised employees he would help them apply for better jobs.

Like Christ, every man shall have a cause in life for which he's willing to die. Our souls are worth dying for, and Christ willingly paid the price of our sins for all humankind. Within ourselves, each of us must determine what path we will follow and, by God's grace, track the route we must. Paul says in Galatians 6:9, "Let us not be weary in well doing: for in the due season, we shall reap if we faint not."

L.E. firmly believed in the adage, "Anything worth doing is worth doing right."

L.E. believed he was reaching a point where the Lord would leave him alone about the preaching revealed to him as a child when he was outside preaching to the seamy beans. So he plunged ahead. How ironic, L.E. chose a preaching style in his union work: he was teaching the gospel of equality, justice, fairness, and humanity.

L.E. was triumphant, winning the race for union president. People said the candidate was an influencer and had a strong presence. He made the union colleagues dream of having more and want to stand up for their rights.

The union swore in L.E. as president of Colored People's Local Union #6131 in January 1961. John F. Rucker, about twenty-five years older than L.E. with a cool head, was vice president. Rucker had been a janitor for a long time with the company, and he was thrilled to give L.E. ample support.

Lawrence H. Randle was the treasurer. He was a strong and quiet family man. Randle's family attended Mt. Calvary church, too, becoming lifelong, trusted friends. The carpool's friend and joker, Ulysses A. Axiel, was the union's chief steward, their contracts' enforcer, and the meeting openings' leader.

L.E. immediately began his letter-writing campaign to company division heads and Mr. Joseph Beirne, C.W.A. president, asking for their support in allowing people of color to apply for craft jobs. L.E. desired to fulfill his commitment to his cohorts and elevate them in the job market as part of the civil rights movement. Therefore, he requested a meeting to discuss policy changes to secure promotions for minorities stuck in house-service positions.

The union officers of local #6131 gathered before all company conferences, and L.E. sincerely desired their etiquette to be impeccable. Being prepared for gatherings meant wearing suits. L.E. always wore suits and dress shoes; he loved silk socks. He informed the men that their journey toward racial integration wouldn't be easy. Therefore, they needed to dress professionally. Also, L.E. required they arrive early for their meetings.

L.E. said, "I'd rather be an hour early than a minute late."

The phone company's South Texas territory covered the major cities from Laredo to Houston and Austin to Corpus Christi. The headquarters were in Houston. The division level was as high as one could go in San Antonio. The division leads were Mr. C.C. Pervier, Division Plant Manager; Mr. Haywood, Traffic Manager; Mr. L.H. Hudson, Commercial Manager; lastly Mr. Hughes, Accounting Manager. These were all middle-aged white conservative men. L.E. doubted they made integration decisions, though upper management agreed to an audience. So at least it was a start.

L.E. concentrated his energies on his bold integration agenda. First, he sat at his blue Underwood typewriter in the black case, which Essie had given him for Christmas. He had learned where the letters were on the typewriter while at St. Philips Junior College. He now typed faster but still with his forefingers. Despite his technique, the typewriter became a tremendous asset to him. L.E. called the typewriter "Old Faithful."

He typed letters to the Southwestern Bell division heads, sharing his vision. He also typed similar letters to the men he saw as his allies: M.LK., President J.F.K., and R.F.K. The responses from the division heads were prompt and cordial, agreeing to a meeting.

While awaiting the green light for union meetings with the division heads, L.E. stayed busy. He assisted union supporters and the community in registering to vote. Using his photographic memory, L.E. educated others on the correct answers. When an individual was ready to sign up,

L.E. went with them for support. After the person concluded they couldn't remember the answers, L.E. acted like he needed to vote.

Moreover, he would not put his name on the paper if a test were required. Once the moderator wasn't watching, he assisted his protégé with the answers or switched forms. L.E. then rose, ripped up his test paper, and left, stating he had changed his mind. In San Antonio, L.E. also used this tactic in travel to Houston, Corpus Christi, and Austin. L.E. went on different days of the week and at other times.

A San Antonio moderator recognized him when he and a lady union member arrived. A young girl was at the counter; L.E. hadn't seen her before. So he and his union member entered and asked to register to vote. The teen told both of them that a test must be successful before voting. L.E. agreed, and she placed the test on the worktop.

No sooner had he picked the test off the large surface than a skinny young moderator with black cat glasses and a chain that hung from them to her mid-section appeared from the side door at the end. She garnished a high bouffant hairdo and smirked.

The lady walked over to him and scoffed, "Hadn't you been here before?"

"Yes. Except, I didn't pass." L.E. replied.

She chuckled softly. "No, I don't think so. You need to leave, and your friend can take the test alone."

"Ma'am, no law exists stating no one else can be present when registering to vote. No law says you have to pass a test before registering to vote either."

"Oh, you one of them smart, uppity 'N's, huh?" Then, leaning on the counter and looking L.E. up and down, she smirked; and said with an attitude of entitlement. "Leave right now, or I'll call the police."

L.E. gritted his teeth, silently bounced his fists on the counter, and repeated that no such law existed.

The woman became angry and got closer to L.E., "I said leave now, or your ass is going to jail, N*. Now, get!"

L.E. blew air out and turned to his union membership. "I'll wait for you outside. Don't worry, and you'll do fine."

The woman passed the test. After that, L.E. realized he had to change his dressing style for future voter registration attempts. Thankfully, segregation laws weren't on the books in San Antonio. Still, the police enforced segregation.

In March 1961, L.E. was granted an audience by the division heads Pervier, Haywood, Hudson, and Hughes. He discussed his plan at their union meeting. The issues for dialogue were that Bell was not complying with the federal government requirements for unbiased employment.

The people of colors' union #6131 wanted to apply for all craft positions if they qualified. They also wanted equal pay and desired the unions to be combined and have their conferences together. The association needed to apply sustained pressure to the Southwestern Bell Company until a sufficient confirmed resolution occurred. All the members agreed.

Accompanied by John F. Rucker, the union's vice president, the group entered and took their seats on one side. Ulysses Axiel, the chief steward, attended many consultations with L.E. and Rucker. Ulysses stood at the door. As president, however, L.E. did the majority of the talking.

The vast room was on one of the upper levels. Along one wall were expansive, seamless windows that overlooked west downtown, facing the setting Sun. L.E. walked over and stood with his arms crossed, staring out those windows. He wondered, a beautiful sight to behold. *Why do I have to ask for permission to achieve better?*

With his Local union, #6131 officers were already in the conference room filled with stale smoke, sitting at a massive mahogany table, a full fifteen minutes awaiting the division manager's arrival. There was a glass pitcher of water, so cold condensation was dripping on the outside, and four glasses were sitting on the table on an oval, shiny silver tray. Eventually, the four-division management team entered, nodded, and took their seats opposite the union members. They poured a glass of water and lit their cigarettes, not offering either to the colored union members.

Mr. Haywood, the division traffic manager, was straightforward about implementing L.E.'s integration policy. He stated reservations about hiring Negroes in any telephone craft positions, including operators, due to their proximity to the white operators. Haywood was concerned about Negroes' ability to work smoothly with whites. Yet, to his credit, Haywood never said it wouldn't happen.

L.E. asked Haywood if he had ever had a housekeeper, a cook, or a yardman. Because when those people of color were in his home next to his wife, helping prepare a meal, no one was worried about getting along. He further interjected that people of color always had to restrain themselves and work smoothly with whites. There was no reason people of different genders, races, cultures, or religions couldn't co-exist in a work environment peacefully. They've done this all their lives, after all.

A better-paying position would make the task easier, not harder. In addition, it provided an opportunity to allow employees to feed their families, which led to happier humanity and, thereby, a better community. Finally, L.E. told them that knowing a person made working with them easier; at the time, white folks were afraid of what they didn't understand.

Because management didn't flatly reject their proposals throughout several meetings, L.E. and his fellow union officers felt uplifted. L.E. was aware the struggle would be hard but now more confident the goal was achievable. He repeated the same information over and over again to the division heads.

L.E. gave his team a pep talk, reminding them, "We need to be grateful things are as well as they are. Let's keep pushing."

He continued his letter-writing strategy, asking Southwestern Bell management to consider house-servicemen and women for higher-paying craft jobs, similar to all other employees. L.E. also shrewdly watched its daily job announcements to know their employment needs. Then, finally, he entered the office. Mrs. Mitchell was sitting at her desk behind the counter doing paperwork. She peered over her glasses, watching L.E. walk over to the job board, and shook her head.

He asked Mrs. Mitchell if the human resource office in St. Louis would get involved. She assured him it was doubtful, but they would make decisions based on each district's union heads' recommendations. Afterwhich, however, he was welcome to write them again.

L.E.'s determination and dedication escalated. He moved "Old Faithful" down to the union hall on Saturdays to type letters for every house-service person who desired a better-paying job in the craft ranks. During his time there, he supported voter registration. L.E. typed over 100 letters for civil rights meetings and job requests. L.E. planned to continue the process until all union member requests were typed and submitted.

After completing other requests, L.E. wrote a letter asking for consideration for a clerk job as a business representative in the Commercial

Department. Since Commercial and Plant were two different departments, there would be a hearing at the headquarters level.

Southwestern Bell organized scheduled hearings, a massive step forward, to begin voluntary integration. John Rucker, vice president; Ulysses Axiel, chief steward; and Mr. Paul Gray, a young white male liaison of the district director for the central C.W.A. National Union, attended with L.E. The three would meet with Mr. Kirkpatrick, the commercial general manager. The area plant personnel supervisor Paul Parker represented the general plant manager.

The meeting began in a very cordial manner and continued to move civilly. For a while, at least. Kirkpatrick stated his position clearly as he viewed it from the Commercial departments' standpoint. Of course, he insisted, they were looking for excellent people only. Although civil, these men gave the impression that they were apathetic to Local #6131's cause. Nevertheless, they were going through the motions, so they had documentation to show the government.

Parker said to L.E., "As far as I care, if I were your supervisor, I would fire you for not doing a respectable job where you are now."

In response, L.E. rapidly stood up and banged his fist on the desk. Then, he said to Parker heatedly, "You smug son of a…how in the Hell can I do any better a job than I'm already doing? The building I'm responsible for maintaining has received the highest rating General Headquarters gives on building inspections, and you can't do any better than that!"

After the exchange, Rucker and Gray led L.E. out into the hallway. With a hand on L.E.'s shoulder, Rucker implored, "Man, you've got to keep your cool. You can't lose it after all of this time. This meeting is your moment to shine. Shoot, this is our moment. You can't let them bastards get your goat. Ain't that what you tell the union members?"

Gray nodded his head fervently.

As L.E. responded, his voice shook with anger. "I know you're right. But he is ragging on my work, man. I'm aware I do an excellent job. Besides, my mother taught me to do my best regardless of my job."

"And? We knew this would happen, L.E.," Rucker said. "He's a racist. So now, take some deep breaths, and we'll go back in when you're ready."

"I want to take care of my family, man. So I can make a better future for my kids. I don't want them to only mop floors because of their beautiful chocolate skin."

"Yeah, man, I know. We all do, and we may complete the journey because of what's happening here. So it'll be okay."

"Yeah, man," Gray interjected. "This road ain't gonna be easy. So what is it, you always say?"

L.E. responded, "Plant a seed of thought to provoke an action of change."

"That's right. You're planting seeds, man. The growth is gonna take time," Gray said.

L.E. cleared his throat and tucked both hands into his pockets.

"You know, there's an adage," L.E. said. "If a dog bites you once, shame on that dog. But, if a dog bites you again, shame on you."

Lifting one side of his lips, L.E. grinned. "Let's go get 'em, fellas. Old Yeller is waiting."

Axiel stood at the door as if a guard on duty, reached over to close the door behind them, and whispered in L.E.'s ear, "Give them racist sons of bitches Hell, L.E."

When the meeting reconvened, Parker returned to the matter of job performance. He insisted the poor appraisal in L.E.'s file meant there was no point in further discussion and suggested L.E. discuss it with his supervisor. Eventually, Parker said the group would meet again in a few months.

L.E. rose to his feet, put his hand to his heart, and looked at each man. "All we're asking for is a chance to compete fairly for positions at this company. The color of a person's skin is no indication of their intelligence. So why are we being denied equal opportunity to live our American dream? Thank you."

Regardless, L.E. knew his supervisor submitted no negative appraisal; that tactic delayed integration efforts. L.E. was aware that employees reviewed and signed their supervisor appraisals, and no such signing had happened. His supervisor later confirmed that no such negative evaluation existed.

Never Quit

Standing firm and moving forward is the only viable option, regardless of its difficulties. You can't go backward and hide your head in the sand because racism or inequality will someday darken your doorstep.

Unfortunately, the world is not fair to everyone that lives in it.
Some have to trudge an uphill battle. They go through
many stressors to fight for what's right. Debt may try
to encompass you, and depression haunts you.

You may rest but never stop.
The end goal is just around the corner
Though it may seem so far away

When hitting the hardest, stick to your fight
It would be best never to quit when a thing appears at its
worst when you're about to have a breakthrough.

Fulfill your purpose in life. Act out of compassion, love, and
kindness, and you're aligned with your true purpose

Sharon Bennett 2019

L.E. Bennett.
President of then Colored
People's Union #6131

Early life, after
marriage

John F. Rucker,
Vice President of
Union #6131

1980's

Earth's Gift   Heaven's Gain

May 22, 1907   July 4, 2007

✞ Scripture ✞

(left) Mr. Ulysses Axiel, Union Sargeant at Arms

(middle) Mr. Lawrence Randle,Union Treasurer and with life-long friend Bennett

(bottom left) Randles's and Wright's with spouses, Bell/AT&T employees, friend's of Bennett.
(right) Sharon with Mr. Randle June 2021

^Dr. Ruth Bellinger

Rev. Dr. Claude Black
right>
and Mr. Gene Coleman
(below left)

**L.E.'s staunch
NAACP and
political
supporters.**

**SNAP News
article
L.E.'s retort to
comments made
at U.P.O
Convention by
Mr. Scott, Jan.
1963.**

greetings from President L. B. Johnson who communicated his apologies for not being able to attend the recent birthday party for Rudy Esquivel.

scenes from the birthday party held for State Representative Rudy Esquivel, in the Villa Fontana, 433 South Alamo, Wednesday March 18, 1964. Top picture (l. to r.) L. E. Bennet, labor man; Gill Pompa, Assistant D. A.; Judge Peter Curry and assistant D. Earl Hill and his wife.

**Birthday Party for state rep. Rudy Esquivel.
L. B. Johnson communicated not being able to
attend.
(Left) L.E.Bennett, Gill Pompa,ADA; Judge P.
Curry (center)and ADA Earl Hill & wife**

94

"Old Faithful," Christmast gift from Essie to type union letters.

Underwood 1960's

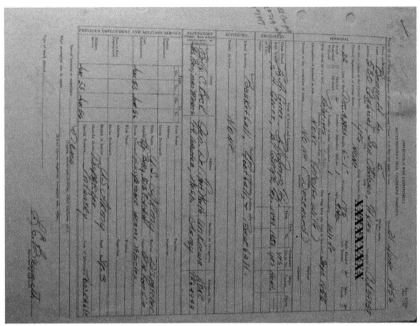

L.E.'s employment application and affadavit
1956

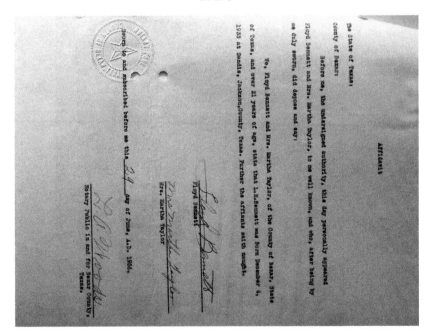

12

Heartbreak

L.E.'s intuition told him that now was the time to agitate more to move forward with the vision for integration. After the letter writing, what tactic should be next? More pressure needed to be applied. Options existed, such as picketing or asking customers to disconnect their phone services.

On a warm Sunday afternoon in spring 1961, L.E. and his mother, Anice, watched the kids play in the backyard while Essie and baby Kenneth napped. L.E. articulated to her his struggles with the corporation and sleepless nights. His head was full of what had taken place and plans. L.E. expressed to Anice his anger over being undervalued by white people at work and how he had to control himself from losing his temper. L.E. wondered how he would shake things up without risking the small advancements the union had already gained.

Anice told her son some wise but straightforward advice: state the facts and stick with those points. Nothing more and nothing less. She suggested future job letters include some history about the employees who wished to rise through the ranks. L.E. decided what he needed to do. Number one was to list their desires in order of importance, but another option was to give practical examples to which anyone could relate.

Therefore, one of L.E.'s plans was for every union member to complete a form. Each employee's name, position, and office they worked, as well as any positives or negatives, were added. L.E. told them to have management write down a compliment on their work, as they would do for a negative.

Their secretary was to put the information on a spreadsheet for him. When presented with an employee's example of why they couldn't be advanced, L.E. would immediately retort with any corrections. Thus, they became more than a name for the company. No management wanted to openly say they did not promote someone because of their skin color. Therefore, L.E. painted these men into a corner with basic common sense. L.E. was like a lawyer declaring his case with exact precision.

L.E. would point out that these were loyal, dedicated, and diligent people. They had received regular merit raises. So, they were favorable enough to keep as an employee. If these employees weren't providing excellent service, why weren't they fired? Their work was acceptable for wage increases. So why hadn't they been promoted?

This line of questioning becomes the backbone of L.E.'s new letter-writing and meeting campaigns. Anice sat, nodding her head.

L.E. gazed at his mother and realized something was different about her. She appeared listless. Her visits to the family had decreased.

"Momma, is anything wrong?"

"Don't know, Baby. I seem to be suffering from much indigestion lately."

L.E. suggested his mother go to a doctor for a physical and find out what was happening. Anice said she would go. But, sadly, she never got around to it.

By early summer 1961, when his mother revisited the family, she complained again about stomach issues. L.E. recommended she try exercising more to help stimulate her digestive system. Perhaps walks? Anice got up and walked down to the corner, a short distance. She was exceptionally exhausted upon her return.

L.E. alerted his siblings that their mother needed to visit a doctor because something was wrong. He called Norcie and Martha and asked if they would take Anice to Robert B. Green Hospital for a check-up the following morning. They quickly agreed and picked her up early the following day. As usual, L.E. departed for the Pershing Central Office at 6:00 a.m.

The whole day passed, but L.E. didn't hear a word from his sisters about the matriarch's condition. So after work, he went straight to the hospital. L.E. found his family and mother sitting in the waiting room. Norcie and Martha told him they hadn't seen a doctor yet. Enraged, L.E.

rushed to the receptionist's desk and demanded they summon the nurse in charge.

When the lady came out, L.E. pointed to Anice, now slumping over in the chair, and stated his concern in a growling voice.

"That's my mother. She has been here since 5:30 this morning, and no one has attended to her, yet. I want somebody out here to check on my mother right away!"

The nurse was apologetic and had Anice immediately taken for examination and quickly admitted to the hospital. The situation was indeed grave; the diagnosis was pancreatic cancer and hyperglycemia.

Anice had been in the medical center for twelve days; Rev. B.F. Langham, Anice's pastor from Louise, Texas, visited and prayed. L.E.'s eldest sister, Hattie Mae (Totah), also arrived.

Anice told him, "Reverend, I'm not worried. My life is'n tha hands of God, and my ticket on that ship has already been paid fer. So I' ma be all right. I will not only get ta meet my Maker, but I' ma get to see my loving Dan. Ya know he was my 'N.'"

L.E. visited his mother daily after work. They prayed and sang together. He would tell her about his day, and she told him stories about the family and when he was young. The hospital was still trying to balance her blood sugars and manage her cancer. The medication made her sicker, but she never complained.

On July 30, 1961, a Sunday morning, L.E. awakened early and went to visit his mother. He kissed Essie goodbye and told her he'd meet the family later for church services. L.E. reached the hospital and started down the hallway to his mother's room when Totah approached with tears in her eyes.

L.E. asked her, "What's wrong?"

But in his heart, he already knew.

"Momma left us."

The emotions L.E. experienced were indescribable; he wanted to holler and scream, but his maleness wouldn't allow him to do so. The heart-wrenching pain was unbearable, as if someone had pierced his chest with their fist and yanked his heart out. He held his sister tightly for a while as she wept. Then, tearing himself away, L.E. walked into his mother's room.

L.E. kissed his mother on the forehead and clasped her hands, still warm in death. He gazed at Anice's hands while biting his bottom lip. She had such lovely little fat hands, with curved pinkies. He bent over to kiss his mother's hands that had once cradled him. He thought *she had always comforted and supported him. Maybe if she hadn't had to work so hard*; finally, he wept bitterly, L.E. couldn't hold back any longer. He recalled crying as a sign of weakness to Anice, and she taught her children not to cry in public. A painful lump formed in his throat, and he couldn't move as tears hurriedly rolled down his cheek. Without her, he's lost.

"Oh my God, oh my God! Why?" L.E. cried out. "I can't make it without you, Momma."

She was gone! The beautiful, proud, gentle, sweet woman. The person who struggled so hard to keep the family together after her husband had died. She was now with him. At the age of twenty-eight, L.E. felt like an orphan. Grown, but still so young and under tremendous pressure.

L.E. stood by Anice's bedside, thinking about what a remarkable woman his mother had been. The world needed more Anice Bennetts. She was the "Book of Knowledge" for all his questions. She was his comforter when he was hurt, strength at his weakest moments, and encouragement whenever he had doubts. But now, she was gone. The pillar that the children had once leaned on was now at rest. No matter how hard L.E. tried to stop, the tears streamed down his face. Again, he kissed Anice's face, and those beautiful hands then turned from her and walked away.

I Kissed The Hand That Cradled Me

I kissed the hand that cradled me, that held me whilst I slept;
And spoke soft words of comfort, as deep within I wept.
I stood there by the bedside, her voice now frail and low;

I listened as she told me to weep for her no more.
I kissed the hand that cradled me and whispered in my heart.
Though death would take her from me,

In memory, we'd never part.
I touched her face, still warm in death, as in peace she lay;
and vowed down deep within my heart that we'd meet again someday.

L.E. Bennett August 22, 1961

The family gathered at Norcie's house on Rex St. to make funeral arrangements. L.E. concluded his mother would have a headstone, and the rest of them agreed—services held at Mt. Calvary Baptist Church, with Rev. Langham officiating.

Following the services, they assembled at 1607 Hays Street, where Anice had lived, with Mrs. Watkins, a widow. Mack, Carl, Floyd, and L.E. were standing in the front yard, talking amongst many people in attendance. All of Anice's surviving brothers and sisters came as well.

L.E. leaned over to pluck a daisy out of the ground, picked off some grass, and threw it. Things seemed surreal to him. "Life is too short, just like that daisy," he said. "Isn't it a shame to wait for a funeral like this to get together? We need to start a reunion."

The brothers agreed, and in November 1961, the first Bennett/Parson Family Reunion took place at Norcie's home in San Antonio. (Parson was Anice's maiden name.) Unfortunately, not many came out that first year, but L.E. was determined to make things work, so he and Floyd continued the effort. The second gathering was at Brackenridge Park in San Antonio in November 1962. Subsequently, in July 1963, the third held at Southside Park had a fantastic turnout.

If the location was halfway between Houston and San Antonio, more people could attend without spending much money. So L.E. called Hattie Mae and asked if she would host the fourth family meeting in Louise, and she gleefully accepted.

And so, the first event in Louise was held on July 4, 1964. More of the more prominent families could attend. Hattie made an extra effort to invite other Parson family members, so Louise was a very successful site for the Bennett/Parson/Callies family reunion.

L.E. sent out letters every year, and more and more people responded. The family event flourished and was held every third Saturday in August in Louise unless they decided to do something different since many lived across the United States.

1 3

Tension and Stress

There was no rest for the weary. L.E. resumed writing letters to Southwestern Bell management. In addition, he wrote to J.F.K. and R.F.K., the Attorney General, and, repeating a letter to Mr. Joseph Beirne, president of the Communication Workers of America National Union. The message was the same: please join in the push for granting equal opportunity to all Americans. The C.W.A. must allow eligible non-whites to apply for craft positions. Also, the union for people of color must merge with the white coalition.

J.F.K. kept his campaign promise, too. Shortly after being elected President of the United States, he issued Executive Order 10925. J.F.K. released the order on March 6, 1961, which required government contractors to "take affirmative action to consider applicants and employees during employment without regard to their race, creed, color, or national origin."

R.F.K. responded, agreeing with L.E. The company must honor Executive Order 10925. He urged L.E. to proceed with his campaign efforts. R.F.K. also suggested that L.E. use his letter in meetings with the telephone company. If L.E. made absolutely no headway, the attorney general added that the federal government would step in and enforce J.F.K.'s Executive Order. The word absolutely troubled him.

L.E. was pleased to read the governmental support from the president's brother. Except, L.E. had hoped for a little more. Bar the telecommunication companies and the C.W.A. wanted to comply with the law. They needed to make concrete efforts to abide by the new law. So with the order, R.F.K.'s letter, and the personnel files added to L.E.'s crusade.

L.E. Bennett continued to escalate the unions' campaign. He wrote to critical men in power who could aid in his mission, such as D.L. McGowen, the district director for the C.W.A, based in St. Louis, Missouri; and Mr. Paul Gray, San Antonio's area representative in Houston. Albert Bowles was the local representative.

D.L. McGowen responded first and set up a meeting in Albert Bowle's office for the following week. Bowle's had a magnificent wooden desk, a black leather chair on wheels, and documents strewn around.

The people of color's union #6131 had its members meet a few days before to review options. L.E. reminded his union members they paid dues monthly of fifty cents, just like their white counterparts. Mandating applying more pressure, he wanted to know if they'd agree to picket. Consequently, the responses weren't favorable for picketing.

Walking off the job and picketing was too big of a risk to the union members. They worried about being fired and not having income for their families. Protesting was a risk because, in the 1960s, systematic racism kept many black males from working. Many males had to rely on their wives to bring home a paycheck if there was a strike. Therefore, the members implored their union president to keep working on their schedule.

L.E.'s union's decision was disappointing, but he understood. He was risking everything. If L.E. lost his job, how would he provide for his family? Continuing talks was the best option.

The meeting adjourned, and the members headed out. L.E. exhaled sharply and took a seat. Mr. Lawrence Randle, the treasurer, turned over to L.E.

"L.E., did I tell you about what happened when I mopped the breakroom floors?" He asked.

L.E stopped his deep thoughts. "What? No. No man, what happened?"

"Well, the St. Louis Cardinals baseball team was playing on the television, and Bob Gibson struck a man out."

"Wow, I wish I could've seen that. I'd love to go to a game one day, Randle."

"Yeah, after Gibson struck the guy out, one of the white employees whooped and hollered. Then he said, 'Damn, that 'N' can pitch.' Once he realized I was still there, he apologized for saying 'N.' I told him it was all right. Anyone can slip. Like when I might slip and say redneck, honky, cracker, or peckerwood. He got up and stomped out."

Both men started laughing, and L.E. cheered up. Randle patted him on the back and told him all would be well. The two got up and left for home.

When L.E. arrived for the meeting a few days later, he noticed Mr. McGowen appeared solemn. Mr. McGowen greeted only Mr. Bowles and Mr. Gray at the meeting, avoiding the men whose efforts had brought them together. McGowen, the district director, sat there stiff and frowning.

L.E. began the meeting by stating their requests for equality with craft jobs and pay. The people of color union wanted fair labor practices by allowing colored employees to apply for open craft positions of technicians, installers, operators, and management.

Mr. McGowen was frigid and grunted, "I think the workforce integration will present some sensitive problems." He cited what he deemed potentially explosive situations: Negro Southwestern Bell employees, working as installers, were assigned to go into homes of good white people to set up phones, and many of those white people wouldn't be accustomed to having Negro people come into their homes.

Bowles uttered, "Mr. McGowen, you shouldn't say that."

"I'm in charge here," McGowen growled.

L.E.'s eyes widened as he gasped, but he tempered his reaction and responded calmly. "I have difficulty understanding the logic used here. When people of color were cooks, housekeepers, yardmen, and now letter carriers, they had no trouble going into the homes of white people. What's so strange about a Negro installing a telephone in a house? You do know that our color doesn't rub off, right?"

Bowles and Gray glared on as if unable to stop the interchange, while Randall and Rucker glanced at each other.

Mr. McGowen said those higher-level positions were different, and he didn't understand how a white woman operator would sit all day next to a Negro woman as if they were equal.

"Besides, we won't be able to guarantee the safety of those gals. Who knows whom it may anger to have Negra gals answering the line?"

L.E. ground his teeth and paused for a moment. "You mean it's okay when colored people are in a position of servitude? Like when slavery is taken away with one hand, but sharecropping and Jim Crow instituted with the other?"

"Well, you people keep asking for things. If it's not one thing, it's another. I mean, when will the giving you stuff stop?"

Bowles attempted to interject, "McGowen, maybe we should..."

L.E. cleared his throat. "Firstly, Mr. McGowen, you're not giving us anything. Only a level playing field, fair opportunity, and a good life are what we are asking for; secondly, people of color are brilliant, creative, and dependable. So move out of the way, and we'll get it ourselves; or, is that what you're afraid of?"

Mr. McGowen scoffed and had no immediate response. Instead, after a few moments, he repeated his first statement.

The progress made that day was questionable, but L.E. left management with the assurance that the local union wouldn't stop its quest for equal employment opportunities, even if it involved the federal government. L.E. passed them copies of his letter from RFK, and their eyebrows raised.

When Southwestern Bell merged with the mother company of AT&T, they sent representatives to meet with L.E. late in 1961. L.E. asked that anyone sent needed the authority and desired to make changes.

The next group of representatives appeared primarily cordial, and the conversations were productive. At least L.E. knew where everyone stood. L.E. believed Southwestern Bell/AT&T would pursue equal opportunities under J.F.K.'s Executive Order. Therefore, those company leaders must be the ones who can make decisions.

To L.E., they wasted precious time, and the ongoing employment injustice reflected poorly on the union, denying families an opportunity to earn decent wages commensurate with white employees. Moreover, this inequity would negatively affect generations of people of color, stonewalling their children from achieving higher education, better careers, and higher wages. Finally, the impact on people of color's livelihood wouldn't be positive simply because white people didn't feel ready to give equal opportunity to a person of color.

L.E. was frustrated but not discouraged. In fall 1961, he'd read a lot about a dynamic young minister and wrote for advice. First, he addressed the letter to the Southern Christian Leadership Conference (SCLC): M.L.K.

At the same time, L.E. resolved to utilize every means at his disposal to push the issue of job opportunities with AT&T. Corporations needed full integration, and he started with his employer. The meetings carried on with division-level managers; some went better than others. L.E. was spreading the word like a lay preacher. He's traveling to Harlingen, Brownsville, Houston, Corpus Christi, and Austin, seeking employees eager to prove they deserve better-paying jobs. He was willing to groom them to pursue job vacancies when they came up aggressively.

L.E. continued to collect sheets on each of his union members. They wrote down all the accolades they had received for their work. Then, if anyone brought up an unsatisfactory employee report in the meetings, L.E. could rapidly respond.

Two Mexican Americans from his union were allowed to bid on and interview for Bell craft positions. These two men had near-white complexions and expressed their job conflicts. They wanted better-paying jobs, but what would it be like for people of color? The circumstance irritated L.E. because he determined those men were tokens. Yet, on the other hand, he was concerned about the fury of hate that could pour out on them and if they'd be able to withstand it.

The company thought this action would show they integrated and honored J.F.K.'s Executive Order. But, conversely, it was not enough or in compliance, and L.E. saw through their farce. For L.E., these were days of more deception. First, he got a glimmer of hope that the company was moving closer toward equality; next, nothing happened.

One night, L.E. arrived home exhausted and stressed. Essie had his dinner waiting for him warming in the oven. The kids were playing and chattering, as they usually did. However, L.E. had no patience for noise on this night and demanded the small children's total silence. After a few minutes, the chatter started again; L.E. yanked the belt off his waist to hit the kids.

Sharon, four-and-half years old, was the first to be struck. She jumped so much that the belt wrapped around her arm and flew from L.E.'s hand. Sharon let out a loud squeal when the metal buckle hit her left cheek, causing bleeding. Essie heard the noise, entered the living room, and became hysterical, but she quickly grabbed Sharon, cleaned the wound, and put a bandage on it. Unfortunately, the injury left a scar that looks like Florida turned sideways.

L.E. regretted that moment for years to come. The injury certainly wasn't L.E.'s intention. Instead, he held her precious face between his hands and kissed it, saying, "Baby, daddy's so sorry. I love you."

Sharon smiled, showing her dimples, and said, "Love you, Daddy."

L.E. was only human with immense pressure on his shoulders as he tried to move his little part of the world from darkness into light.

As his union work grew, L.E. realized it was time to get another car. It would save time and money to avoid dealing with the bus and transfers. So he purchased a 1955 red and white Ford Fairlane with whitewall tires and shiny hub caps. While he saved time by not riding the bus for work, Essie also had a car for errands and the kids. Therefore, he drove the family to Mt. Calvary Baptist Church when Sunday mornings rolled around. L.E. felt respectable about taking his family to church. He also took the family to the Lincoln Drive-In some Friday nights and ordered foot-long hot dogs and sodas.

His career and life often kept L.E. away from family, whether school, homework, local politics, working in the union, NAACP meetings, or his everyday job. As a result, scheduling time together was rare. On weekends, the occasional drive-in was L.E.'s way to make amends to the family for offering so little leisure time together.

However, not every free Friday was with his family. Occasionally, L.E. went by The Ice House on Houston Street to get a beer and unwind. A couple of miles from the house, it was a makeshift bar on the east side of San Antonio, and it appeared like a half aluminum and wooden trailer home with one side open to the public. It had old barstools lined in front of a long metal counter with an extended metal footrest. The customers couldn't go inside due to lack of space, but they could see a lit sign with pricing and a wide selection of drink options. The bar also carried candy, ice cream, and sodas.

That night L.E. pulled into a parking space on the curb to grab a beer at The Ice House. Other than a soda, beer was his drink of choice. While reviewing his list of union chores, a man walked up behind him and patted him on his back.

"Hey Daddy-O, what are you doing here?"

L.E. looked up, and it was his brother Floyd (Honey).

With an enormous grin, L.E. got off his barstool and hugged him. "Hey, Honey, I'm so happy to see you. Have a seat and have a drink with me."

Honey sat on a stool, pulled out a cigarette, and lit it. "What are you doing here, Baby?"

"Oh, I'm just trying to relax my mind. Some Fridays are my time to be out. Hey, can I get one of those?"

Stunned, Floyd said, "Sure. But, I thought you stopped smoking?" He handed L.E. a cigarette and lit it for him. "Your night out. Oh, really?" He gestured to the girl for one beer.

"And what about Essie? Does she get her night out too?"

L.E. sighed. "What, man? What are you talking about, Honey?"

Floyd flicked his cigarette ash in the tray nearby. "I'm talking about your wife. She's working hard, just like you are. She's holding you up and carrying the family while you do your union thang. That's boss. We need you to do that work, brother. So don't let up now. Man, you can't go out like this drinking alone. There's an image you must always present. Drink at home or be out with your wife."

L.E. was caught off guard and dazed with the interchange, not knowing what to say. However, he instinctively understood that Floyd was right. They talked about work a bit, joked around, and finished their beers before going home.

"Well, Baby, I'm heading home to my beautiful wife," said Floyd.

"Of course, the beautiful Janie Winters of Corinth Baptist church. You got blessed with that woman," replied L.E.

"We've both been blessed, baby brother. Talk to you soon," yelled Floyd while getting into his car.

You might say L.E. was burning the candle at both ends, and he was still meeting with the CWA union officials and AT&T upper-level management. But, instead of being exhausted, L.E. was excited. It was a thrill, an adrenaline rush because he was helping people, and sometimes he could even see a glimmer of hope. But unfortunately, this double-edged sword kept him from sleeping, and ulcers soon developed.

I Can't Sleep

My heart is troubled. My mind is full
I toss and turn, not knowing which path to take
Every day is a delicate balancing act
Every meeting means people you have to appease

Carefully consider all of your words.
So as not to offend, but they couldn't care less
if I'm offended or demeaned
My shoulders are heavy with the weight
of responsibility

Feed my family, do a great job at work
Continue my education and fight for
equal rights, so that one day we'll all
be able to choose life

Feed my family, do a great job at work
Continue my education and fight for
equal rights, so that one day we'll all
be able to choose life

My first and closest confidant is gone
I mourn her still
Wishing for her advice as I
pray for direction
The burden is so heavy

My stomach burns, and my
chest aches with the stress
They don't know, and they don't care
how things get better, just that they do
The sacrifice is great and
The burden is heavy

Sharon Bennett 2019

14

Run 'N' Run

In summer 1962, the CWA held its annual convention at the Muehlebach Hotel in downtown Kansas City, Missouri, and L.E.'s life was in peril.

The hotel hosted several presidents in a twelve-story brown brick building: Theodore Roosevelt, Woodrow Wilson, Calvin Coolidge, Herbert Hoover, and Harry S. Truman. As a result, the Muehlebach Hotel became known as the White House of the west. Numerous white celebrities also stayed, including Helen Keller, Ernest Hemingway, Babe Ruth, Frank Sinatra, and Bob Hope.

L.E. looked forward to representing local union #6131. He wrote CWA president Joseph Beirne in advance and requested a meeting during the convention. L.E. wanted to speak with Beirne. Having read literature from their CWA president, who campaigned for equality and increased pay for the CWA workers. Beirne gave a supportive impression to the union members and the appearance he would fight for them in social causes.

Joseph A. Beirne's father, the son of Irish immigrants, worked with the union railroad. Beirne grew up in Jersey City, New Jersey. In 1927, he worked for Western Electric, the Bell Telephone System manufacturing division. The Wagner Act passed in 1935, and Beirne, with other employees, began organizing the nation's phone workers. The National Federation of Telephone Workers began in 1938, and Beirne ascended to the C.W.A. presidency by 1943, at age thirty-two.

Educated and well-read, L.E. called and reserved a room for Essie and himself without difficulty. He also purchased train tickets to Kansas City after determining the least expensive way to take a trip. Full of excitement, this train trip would be their first. Essie had never traveled out of state before. Imagine no kids, no meals to prepare, no house to clean on their trip. She would be living the high life.

Finally, the day arrived. L.E. and Essie drove to Houston to visit his brother Mack and his wife, Ruby, Essie's brother Ollie and Jessie, his wife. Soon, they had to go to the train station downtown.

Such a dismal place. The interior had wooden pews with different sections for coloreds, including separate toilet and water fountain areas. When the conductor called, Essie and L.E. walked to the last car. L.E. handed their luggage to the porter, and they boarded the train for Kansas City.

L.E. focused his energy on planning the meeting with Joseph Beirne. He would implore him to use his influence as the white man's union president to help achieve the lofty goal of integration at the phone company. If challenged, L.E. would stress implementing J.F.K.'s Executive Order and the National Union Office's assistance.

L.E. discovered other C.W.A. members aboard. In their train car, with only one other non-white couple, but friendly enough, he shrewdly established a pretty positive rapport with all.

L.E. met a young red-headed man from Waco toward the front of their car. The two began a tremendous conversation about working for the telephone company and living in Texas. However, Red had a craft position with a high school diploma, and L.E., a janitor with an associate's degree and working on his bachelor's. Red appeared empathetic to L.E.'s plight, and L.E. liked him a lot.

The next day, after a few stops, the train pulled into the Kansas City station. A few taxicabs passed the young couple, an unfamiliar situation to L.E. and Essie; finally, one took the Bennetts to the Muehlebach Hotel.

The cab stopped in the back of the hotel and let the Bennetts out. L.E. took their suitcases, and Essie had her train case. She'd never stayed in a hotel before and gazed at the impressive twelve-story brick and stone building with green awnings on top of the first-floor windows.

They went through the back-glass doors to enter the hotel hallway, heading toward the main lobby. The lobby had wooden walls and columns with beautiful crystal chandeliers embellished with gold and highly polished brass accents.

Before reaching the desk, the couple passed an impressive flight of marble stairs. But when they entered the lobby, a humongous wide-sweeping marble staircase with an exquisite rug going up the center, grander than in the movie "Gone with the Wind," greeted them. A lovely giant gold-colored statue with white wings soared at the second level.

An enormous check-in desk anchored the lobby with thick heavy wood and white marble countertops. A skinny white female with wire-rimmed glasses cautiously went over to wait on them at the hotel counter. L.E. smiled and identified himself and his wife, explaining they had a reservation. The young lady glanced around to see if they accompanied anyone else while locating their reservation card. Once she found it, she excused herself to go into an office and speak to an older woman.

She returned to the counter, smiling. "Thank you for waiting. Unfortunately, we seem to be mighty full due to the convention. Is a smaller room, okay?"

L.E. leaned on the counter and smiled. "Well, I made reservations by phone weeks ago for a junior suite. Is the price lower?" L.E. asked.

"Yes, it is."

"We'll take it," he said a bit disappointed.

She rang the bell on the desk, summoning a colored bellhop. The bellboy took the Bennetts back the way they had come in, past the elevators and a mailbox to the first-level marble stairs. The couple glared at each other as they sighed. The bellboy took them up to a room at the end of the hall on the second floor.

Before leaving, he explained that their hotel area was where the help of their white guests stayed and the rules for colored guests at their hotel. For example, they would not be allowed to eat in restaurants outside of the convention, but they may place room service orders or dine elsewhere.

It was a modest room, divided into the living room near the front door and the bedroom in the back, with a bathroom connected. Although clean, neat, and smelling fresh, the furniture and draperies were frumpy browns.

Essie looked forward to a restful break. But L.E. wanted to go to the lobby, looking for colored union members. He met a gentleman who was the President of his local people of colors' union, but they only made small talk. The man didn't have the vitality L.E. looked for in a potential ally in the cause.

Now, 7 p.m. and time for the delegates' dinner. Finally, L.E. would come face-to-face with Joseph Beirne before their scheduled meeting on Saturday. The beautifully decorated ballroom held large round and square tables with an area for the white union members and a smaller section for the colored members who had managed to make the trip. The number of non-white attendees counted as less than ten.

Finely pressed white linen tablecloths draped down, gently kissing the hardwood floors. White china and elegant sterling silverware place settings graced the tables' top, reflecting diners' images. The crystal goblets and glasses awaited to quench the guests' thirst. Each table boasted a colorful floral arrangement which filled the hall with a seductive scent. Matching florals adorned the walls at evenly spaced locations. Soothing music played lightly over the loudspeakers, and the ballroom was full of exciting, indistinct chatter.

Sharply dressed, L.E. and Essie had on their Sunday best. The convention was their time to shine, and that night, the pre-convention dinner. L.E. prepared to make a lasting impression by donning a beautiful black suit. In addition, he had a black tuxedo for Saturday night— borrowed, of course. His black wingtips spit-shined like mirrors.

Essie had a shiny royal blue rayon dress which fitted her every curve and went down midcalf, including ruching under her breast line. The navy-blue heels highlighted her already full and shapely legs. Tomorrow night she would wear a gold sleeveless dress with a pale three-quarter sleeved organza overlay, tied at the waist with a wide gold ribbon, and matching shoes. Like her mother-in-law, Anice, Essie could sew well, one of the many things Anice taught her before passing.

The young couple walked around the large crowd, introducing themselves to other delegates. For the most part, folks gawked at L.E. and Essie like crazy, and many wouldn't shake their hands. Nonetheless, L.E. wanted to get acquainted with more people.

"Damn, Essie. These folks act like we're going to steal their wallets or something."

"Yeah, I noticed."

Finally, L.E. located the people he had met on the train, including the red-headed man. Some were friendly. Also, others who had been considerate on the train acted coldly at dinner.

Then, L.E. identified Albert Bowles, Paul Gray, and D.L. McGowen. After a few minutes of casual chatter with Bowles and Gray, Bowles offered an introduction of L.E. to Mr. Beirne, the National President.

At last, the hour had come. L.E. grinned, filled with expectations of meeting this gentleman with whom he had only corresponded. Politically active, Beirne worked hard for his union members. L.E. was eager to personally ask for assistance in the plight for equality in Texas.

Bowles led L.E. and Essie over to a group of men talking and laughing. Bowles touched one of the gentlemen on the back. When the man turned around, L.E. immediately recognized him from a C.W.A. photo. Unsurprisingly, the people of color union members' pictures and names weren't in the union booklet. Beirne was about an inch or two shorter than L.E., with black-framed glasses and straight, dark thinning hair slicked back with some greying on each side from ear to temple. Mr. Beirne turned around and stood stoic with a cigarette in one hand and a drink in the other.

Albert Bowles said, "Mr. Beirne, I want you to meet L.E. Bennett, president of Local #6131, in San Antonio, Texas."

L.E. smiled and extended his hand to shake Mr. Beirne's.

Mr. Beirne stared L.E. dead in the eyes. He didn't take his hand, and he didn't smile. Instead, Beirne grunted, "Hmph, we've corresponded. There'll be no integration." He turned his back to L.E., resuming his conversation.

Both Bowles and Gray's mouths dropped open, and they apologized to L.E as they stumbled over their words.

Being humiliated and snubbed as though he were nothing infuriated L.E. Plus, kicking that man's butt right in the ballroom wouldn't help the cause. Beirne's support of social causes, letters, and radio interviews were for whites and non-inclusive of blacks. L.E. began to wipe his forehead, pull his ear and pull his hands in and out of his pockets. Essie gently grabbed L.E.'s hand to lead him away from Beirne.

"What an asshole! A damn asshole," L.E. muttered through gritted teeth.

"I understand, baby. Calm down."

"Why in the Hell do I always have to be the one to calm down? I'm sick and tired of calming down." L.E. griped.

Essie glanced at him from the corners of her eyes. "Let's go on to our table, Daddy."

"Honey. I'm very sorry. It wasn't for you."

"Oh, I know. And, you know I don't curse. So, don't let it happen again."

The couple returned to their table to calm down. L.E. was already thinking about what could be said to Beirne tomorrow at their scheduled meeting.

He rehearsed his lines to Essie. "I'm paying my hard-earned money to help pay your salary. You are a sorry son of a gun. You may be high in the eyes of others, but I just lost respect for you."

Essie gently rubbed his arm and kissed him on his dimple, saying to L.E., "Sounds excellent to me, Honey. Let's sit down."

C.W.A. national president Joe Beirne didn't attend the prescheduled integration meeting the next day; Instead, he sent his executive vice president, Glenn Watts, initially deemed an insult.

"L.E., I believe in your cause, and I will help you," Watts said.

It was hard for L.E. to imagine someone paid to represent your best interests could behave with such blatant disrespect. Then, of course, the big wigs of the Bell/AT&T companies would smile and tell the federal government they were doing everything for employment equality through the C.W.A. But what they meant was equality in jobs for white Americans.

He and Beirne never directly spoke or corresponded again. However, Mr. Glenn Watts turned out to be a gentleman. He shook L.E.'s hand and said it was nice to meet him. Watts assured L.E. that he agreed with the plan to have equality for all union members and would be more than happy to work with him to achieve it. Thrilled to hear this from Watts, a man who hadn't been on his radar before, encouraged, L.E. began to smile.

But, he was an Ally of high position in the union. However, L.E. was still upset with Beirne. Beirne would only come around when it was advantageous for himself.

Under his breath, he stated, "Every dog has his day. And you will have yours, Mr. Beirne."

L.E. squelched his anger and focused his energies on the convention.

Instead, he would advance his agenda by talking with fellow attendees. Saturday evening, the hall was full of people, chattering loudly. Microphones had been installed throughout the ballroom floor, allowing union delegates to voice concerns. That would be L.E.'s opportunity, he decided.

When it was time for members to speak, L.E. approached a microphone and patiently waited his turn. He was the only black who stood to speak. All the delegates, representatives, and directors were there, including his new nemesis Beirne.

As he waited for recognition at the microphone in the black dining section, L.E. thought to himself about making his statement. Starting, he would greet everyone. Then tell the convention and Beirne exactly how he felt and what a disservice they were to the C.W.A. L.E. wanted to emphasize his local #6131 minority members and others; we're paying the same membership dues and deserved equal union representation. Minorities must be allowed to bid for craft jobs. Also, earn support from their union.

Looking Beirne dead in the eyes, the man who had disrespected him, L.E. planned to say, *"It's a sad day in Hell when a union has a president who gladly takes your money into his pockets but acts as though you don't exist. Maybe this union needs a different president representing all members, not just some. But, like it or not, the President of the United States signed an Executive Order, stating any company doing business with the Federal Government will have to abide by it. So now's a new day. We demand change, and we want it now."*

But while other delegates were recognized and spoke, L.E. was not acknowledged, not allowed to verbalize feelings or share the plan's specifics. L.E. attempted to express his viewpoints, but the microphone was off, and there wasn't a switch. So instead, L.E. gazed over to Beirne, smirking and inhaling long on his cigarette.

L.E. believed it was a deliberate act, revenge because of all his strategizing and agitation to promote people of color. Of course, he would never know for sure, but he pledged never to allow that humiliating episode to hinder the unions' ambitions.

The convention weekend drew close after more meetings, events, and meals.

The following Sunday afternoon, the red-headed man L.E. met on the train and went to the hotel cafe for a relaxing drink and meal. Several union members were already seated in varied areas of the eatery.

The café was full of smoke. A few men at one table were in deep conversation. As Red approached the counter, a short, portly bald man at that table called him over to sit with them. He appeared to be in his early forties.

The bald man beckoned to Red. "Hey there, buddy. Are you enjoying the convention?"

"Yeah, I am. But, as conventions go, that's all right."

Pulling out a chair next to him, he said, "Well, take a load off. We're just talking over some union business."

"Yep, take a load off," slurred a tall, slender man with freckles and blue eyes. He appeared more like a high school student.

The men appeared drunk to Red. They seemed to be devising a plan of some sort. An average-built man with blonde hair and a potbelly leaned back in his chair, smoking a cigarette as he gave Red the once-over. He puffed on the cigarette again and took a drink. Then, squinting his eyes, he put the cigarette on the ashtray.

To Red, this blonde man was the ring leader. He surveyed the others and began to speak. The blonde man talked about how the 'N's should be glad they allowed them to come to the convention. Moreover, he guessed the C.W.A. had to recognize them since they paid monthly dues.

The potbelly blonde man was in his late forties to early fifties, leading these other two around by the nose. He continued to say it was enough to have 'N's here—but to have to eat with them, too! Appalled at their language, Red was about to excuse himself when he witnessed something interesting.

A young waitress came to the table to take Red's order, and he asked for scotch on the rocks and a ham sandwich with their soup of the day. She reviewed his order and checked if the other gentlemen wanted anything else. As they glared at her, the waitress thanked them and walked away.

The short bald man said, "What's the name of that tall 'N' from Texas? You know the one that Mr. Bowles introduced to Beirne?"

"It's Bennett," said the blonde man. "He is a problem."

Red asked, "Oh, how is he a problem?"

The blonde man took a long drag from his cigarette, Squinting as if irritated by his production of smoke; subsequently, clearing his throat, he responded. "He thinks he's smart; plus, he tried to meet with Beirne. He's the one that's been doing that civil rights bullshit in and trying to get 'N's better jobs. Jobs that belong to us."

The other two males nodded and called for another round of drinks.

"We got something for uppity, 'N's, though," said the tall, slender, freckled, blue-eyed man.

"Oh, what's that?" asked Red.

"We heard about all the phone calls and assistance he's getting to pressure the company for these higher-paying jobs. So, we'll wait for him in front of the hotel. Next, when he comes out, we'll get him into a car and take him to a party," said the slurring slender, blue-eyed man with freckles.

"A party?" Red inquired.

"Yeah, a ball-busting party. We'll beat the Hell out of him, show him some manners. Also, take his balls," said the blonde-headed man, grinning.

"He has a wife," Red said.

"Well, if that little pickaninny gets in our way, we'll deal with her, too!" the short bald man growled.

"Yeah, plus, we have a couple of other guys to help us," the tall, freckled man slurred.

"Well, she's gorgeous and fair-skinned. I wouldn't mind a little alone time with her," the blonde man said with a sly grin.

The blonde man explained that he got Bennetts late checkout time from the front desk because of a midnight train departure. So, they'd wait outside the hotel's front for L.E. and his wife. Supposedly, the couple came by train, and he'd be too arrogant to go to the back, he sneered. The blonde man and the bald man would have a gun. The skinny man with freckles and another guy would be in his car waiting for the signal down the street.

Red had to warn L.E. without being found out. When the waitress delivered his meal, he steadied his breathing and ate. At the same time, he tried not to throw up as the others' continued offensive speech. He rose once he completed his meal and said he needed a nap. He shook each man's hand and excused himself.

L.E. and Essie were packing for the train scheduled to leave at midnight. Suddenly a rap came at the door. It was the friendly young red-haired gentleman from the train, Red. His face was pale, and he wrung his hands together.

"L.E., some union hotheads are in the cafe, and they are talking about teaching you a lesson for that mouth of yours."

L.E. invited Red in, but he peered over L.E.'s shoulder and saw Essie. Declining entry into the room, he gestured for L.E. to step out. Red started to rattle off when he got to the restaurant, the seat initially chosen, what items he ordered, and how he got nauseous. L.E. could see it was nervous energy and thought it funny. Then Red explained what the group in the eatery had planned. He urged the couple to leave early to avoid harm. The men took a couple more minutes talking about the drunken ignorance of the diner zealots.

L.E. extended his hand to thank Red, saying, "Thank you so much for your kindness. You're a good man. I'd be missing out on a world of wonder if I thought everyone was the same."

L.E. closed the door and peeked at the love of his life, still at the bed packing. He decided not to share news of the impending danger.

He did believe that if anyone tried to harm his wife, they would have to kill him first. L.E. looked at his watch and calculated they had a few hours before they were due at the Union Depot train station.

He approached Essie and gently kissed her on the neck, saying, "Hey Honey, would you like to see a movie instead of sitting around the room?"

"Yes," Essie squealed. She jumped up, kissed him on the cheek, and quickly grabbed the newspaper to check the listings. The Regent Theatre near the hotel showed 'Adrian's Messenger' at 8 p.m. Neither one of them knew anything about the movie but decided to try.

It didn't start for a few hours, but the longer L.E. sat in his hotel room, the angrier he became. Finally, he decided it was best to leave even earlier and go for a bite before the movie.

With clenched fists, he muttered, "This is the kind of shit that makes you want to kill a son of a bitch."

L.E. never spoke at the convention and wondered if those angry men got information from the union president Beirne.

"You say something, Daddy?"

"Yes, let's get our bags and get the Hell out of here. And nobody had better say a word to me unless it's goodbye," he told Essie.

They checked out about 5 p.m. without incident and hailed a cab to the restaurant from the hotel's back. The bellhop recommended a sweet spot to eat close to the theater. The meal was excellent home cooking, and L.E. was glad it was only a weekend trip, and they had only the little bags. They strolled to the theater, explored around town, and window-shopped along the way. L.E. bought the movie tickets, found seats in the colored section, and enjoyed the film.

L.E. and Essie then took a cab to the train station, arriving about an hour before their train departure. After L.E. checked in and received tag receipts for their luggage, the couple sat on one of the long wooden pews in the colored section.

L.E. crossed his legs and started shaking his foot. He repeatedly peeked at the station's astronomical clock and raised the cuff on his crisp white dress shirt to view his wristwatch. Essie read an old magazine left on the bench, glancing at L.E. but said nothing.

The announcement blared over the speakers to begin boarding. L.E. quickly assisted Essie to stand, grabbed their luggage, and went to the platform. He handed the porter their two small suitcases, tipped him, and helped Essie up the train steps.

The colossal train had the locomotive, the restaurant car, the sleeper car, one with ample leg space, and a long aisle with seats by twos. They boarded the last train car and headed to the "Colored Section."

The train whistle shrieked, and a man yelled, "Last call, all aboard." A conductor was coming through to check tickets.

"Oh my God," Essie shouted with cheeks in her hands. "I left my train case on the bench."

"Essie, no," L.E. whined as he hopped up to jump off the train.

"Hey?" the conductor yelled.

"Where is ya goin', brother?" asked the porter.

"Wait for me. My wife left her case," L.E. yelled.

He quickly jetted into the station, grabbed the case, and headed back to the train.

The train began to pull out. Hearing yelling as L.E. exited the station and glanced left. Approaching the ramp was the drunken crew. Still in shape, L.E. ran for the train that was advancing.

"Go, man, go," shouted the porter.

L.E. grabbed the rail and jumped onto the train. The conductor assisted L.E. by his arm and quickly closed the door.

"Man, you like to play it close, don't you?" the conductor laughed.

L.E. stumbled to his seat and flopped in. He handed Essie her case and, leaning forward, stared out the window. A group of white men without luggage ran down the platform screaming obscenities. They saw L.E. at the train window and began pointing and cursing.

Essie looked at L.E. with her mouth open. L.E. casually shrugged his shoulders and leaned back, more steadfast to finish what he had started. Essie never said anything about the matter, but she was keenly aware of their narrow escape.

All at once, Red appeared at L.E.'s seat. He expressed relief that L.E. had heeded his warning and left the hotel early.

"Man, I bet you were a great athlete in school." Subsequently, Red shook L.E.'s hand and bowed with a big grin at Essie. Then he went back to his seat.

L.E. and Red would never see each other again. Nor did L.E. remember the man's real name. Regardless, he would always be grateful for the warning that likely saved Essie's and his lives.

The Bennetts returned to Houston without further incident and headed for El Campo to reunite. A couple more days were spent with Essie's parents and listening to their kids' chatter about their days on the farm, feeding the chickens, slopping the hogs, chasing geese, playing stickball, and lying with their Granddad Dave Jones in the hammock, looking up at the stars.

Know, Listen, Remember

Know when to stand your ground, know when to hold still
know when to forge ahead
learn when to speak, learn when to listen,
learn all you can from everyone

Remember, a faithful Christian hates no one, is compassionate, and
applauds your success, rather than being envious

Sharon Bennett 2000

15

I Need A Little Help

On the drive back to San Antonio, L.E. wondered what had gone wrong with his hopes and dreams for a successful convention. He hadn't yet heard back from M.L.K, but he hoped a letter offering some guidance would be at the house. He hoped the help would be forthcoming to deal with the thwarted process of moving house-service people to better paying jobs. Of course, he was dissatisfied, but his resolve couldn't wane. As the son of Dan and Anice Bennett, two highly influential people, he refused to let any stumbling blocks stand in his way for long.

L.E. decided he would have to be more determined than ever to continue the mission and achieve affirmative action goals with J.F.K.'s Executive Order 10925 for equality in employment.

Mr. Coleman suggested L.E. speak with Dr. Ruth Bellinger, his landlord, a prominent local obstetrician. Their father was Charles Valmo Bellinger, another more influential black newspaper publisher. A millionaire who donated large sums of money to Santa Rosa Hospital so minorities would receive medical care. Coleman explained that Dr. Ruth Bellinger had the pull with the local National Association for the Advancement of Colored People (NAACP). She could get directly involved in L.E.'s battle for equality. Well aware of her status on the board, L.E didn't consider telling the NAACP and asking for help because their plate was packed, and he didn't want to be a burden. But, without assistance, no one could make real change in racism, equal employment, and affecting people's lives. It was time to get his fellow members involved.

On 1314 Ervin Street, L.E. and Mr. Coleman met with Dr. Bellinger at Bennetts' home, and she readily agreed to lend direct assistance. L.E. would continue to address the problem from the inside. Dr. Bellinger, Mr. Coleman, Rev. Claude Black of Mt. Zion First Baptist Church, and the local NAACP would pursue the problem from the outside.

L.E. had written a letter in care of Ebenezer Church in Atlanta, Georgia, earlier in the winter of 1962. As an NAACP member, he vocalized company union goals and status and asked for feedback on strategies. Dr. Bellinger also encouraged L.E. to write M.L.K again. She and Rev. Claude Black added their input, plus L.E. must add his NAACP membership. In addition, they would assist each other with campaigns, speeches, and protests.

A marked lack of employment equality activity existed from Mr. Haywood, AT&T. Therefore, L.E. decided to find some further outside agitation. In the summer of 1963, Bennett contacted his friend, Mr. Eugene Coleman of San Antonio's SNAP newspaper, black-owned and operated—and asked for his editorial assistance again with showcasing the union's employment desegregation efforts.

In addition, he wanted to contradict statements made in July 1963 by a local school teacher and Connally campaign supporter, Mr. Joe Scott. The U.P.O. had a convention at which Joe's supportive campaigning was honored. The U.P.O., United Political Organization, was a group of conservative elite African Americans and Connally backers for governor who began the group after January 1963 in Houston, Texas. In addition, U.P.O. worked to silence the outward social struggles and denounce the loud black unionist.

Scott used that platform to attack black activists partnered with organized labor. He was saying to hell with local and state coalitions because if people of color could rise to government offices, surely they could gain higher-leveled employment. For L.E., Joe and a group leader, a Houston attorney, were self-serving pawns for the U.P.O. taking handouts with unfulfilled promises.

Essentially, the men had different perspectives of the same coin. L.E. felt that the primary focus was to gain better employment and financial security for black families because none could gain loans or own businesses without sufficient income. Without the benefit of family wealth and medical or legal education from Nothern states, how could employees commence major industries on small wages? And, working through the union would help people achieve advancement and job security. But on the other hand, Joe Scott saw unions as a hindrance without upward mobility for blacks, and they couldn't achieve monetary independence without being bosses of their businesses and hiring within the black communities.

Mr. Coleman introduced L.E. to the Masons and Eastern Star organizations. Civic and political-minded, L.E. and Essie joined and became active members for several months. They felt masonry provided the best means for perfecting humanity. The order aspired to attain its ideals by creating an international organization that extended brotherly love, relief, and truth to its members. No wonder L.E. had an interest.

The NAACP began making repeated phone calls to the telephone company management and followed up with letters. Dr. Bellinger and Rev. Black also attended company meetings with L.E. Rev. Black insisted they include train porters, cooks, waiters, hotel bellhops, housekeepers, lumber yards, and ironworks in their campaigns. In addition, they reached out to local businesses that employed blacks. Having an educated and intuitive member within local companies was perfect for integration tactics, and the phone company with the train corporations were huge targets.

The division plant manager turned his meetings with local #6131 over to the division plant personnel supervisor, Harper Nations. Colleagues saw Mr. Nations as a man one could talk to but not expect a lot. After all, he needed to protect the company and maintain its status quo. Surprisingly, Nations became an ally to L.E. and proponents of equality for people. L.E. always laid out the A-B-C's, why the balance was necessary, and no valid reason to deny upward movement. When L.E. attended a meeting, Nations reaffirmed what L.E. said and gave examples of why delaying upward mobility to non-whites would be a black eye on the company's image.

While L.E. tried to fight the good fight for employees, not everyone understood his campaign, afraid of management blowback. Occasionally, the same people L.E. wanted to help would say hurtful things. One such person was Ned Cox. He and others stated that L.E. caused trouble for everyone and only attempted to get attention. Soon many shared that opinion and started to ignore L.E.

Most white employees would whisper and glare at L.E., who rarely spoke against what the colored union members tried to achieve. Some whites said they understood a person wanting better things in life. Yet, conversely, at the same time, they feared losing their jobs to people of color.

L.E. finally received significant support in his battle: a response arrived in early 1963 from M.L.K. The letter advised him to remain calm; some of his people would be against him and afraid of losing their jobs, and some whites would not consider supporting him. M.L.K. urged L.E. to increase his support base by gathering friends, family, and church members. He also suggested L.E. plan a nonviolent march to bring together advocates for equality in employment—even to put the problem in the public eye.

The following week, L.E. worked to widen his campaign. He told Harper Nations, division plant personnel supervisor, "The company shouldn't only consider San Antonio-based jobs for advancement, but any jobs within the district. The local #6131 will be glad to review job opportunities for non-white employees anywhere in Texas."

L.E. added, "If there are any viable openings, and no one else will take the job, I will, rather than see the job go unfilled by a colored union member."

Not a tactic offered by M.L.K., but one in which L.E. firmly believed. He understood that he couldn't lead unless he were willing to follow his advice, even if it was a personal sacrifice. So it would not be long before L.E. could stand behind his words.

Not every black employee at AT&T desired to be open about their desires to move into a better position. Many elderly members remained concerned about problems on the job with white employees. Also, some employees thought to let the union work for them, but they did not want to involve themselves in the union. If the ax fell, the prominent fighters would lose their jobs first, and those who hung back would bear no consequences. Few people of that mentality subsisted. Nevertheless, the public considered them the majority: people of color not satisfied with minimal wages and non-skilled work didn't want to upset the apple cart.

The battle went on. L.E.'s school grades slipped, reflecting the wear and tear on him mentally and physically. Then, in May 1963, the news televised the horrors of Eugene "Bull" Connor and his water hoses turning on blacks in Birmingham, Alabama.

The Selma march was the talk of the town at work and NAACP meetings. But, sadly, some local union members attended and returned with the police and public bigotry tales. This public display of hatred disgusted L.E. to no end. But things turned out to be just the break the movement needed to get prominent people involved.

L.E. had difficulty sleeping and already drank Pepto-Bismol by the bottle. Nevertheless, nausea and burning sensations in his stomach persisted, even after he stopped eating jalapeños. Ultimately, Dr. Stanley admitted L.E. to the hospital with an ulcer, exhaustion, and dehydration diagnoses. On a regimen of medication and rest. The doctor demanded he rests until an improvement in L.E.'s physical condition.

After just one day in the hospital, L.E. asked his wife, Essie, to bring him "Old Faithful," his blue Underwood typewriter, and his school and union books.

L.E. resumed phone calls and letter writing from his hospital bed with enthusiasm. But he became outraged when Dr. Stain made rounds and found L.E. sitting in bed with his typewriter and papers everywhere.

Pointing his forefinger, Stain bawled out his patient, asking how the activist expected to recuperate if he still worked as hard as he always did. The doctor flushed with anger and told L.E. to have Essie come to collect "Old Faithful" and all the paper and take them home. Then he stormed out of the room. L.E. followed the doctor's orders.

When discharged from the hospital, L.E. sensed a surge of rejuvenation.

But, of course, he was back to the old grindstone not long after. Again, politicians and union workers better known on the local and state political scenes would support and assist. They had to be able to connect L.E.'s name with the integration efforts.

L.E. attended the birthday party for state representative Rudy Esquivel, where L.B.J. apologized for not participating in the festivities. Judge Curry and Gill Pompa, A.D.A., were present, as well. The political involvement kept him going, attending one function after another to shine more light on their union cause. With every day, L.E. gained growing support from key players in town. He participated in more state conventions and scheduled more meetings with the telephone company, including negotiations to integrate the telephone operators.

In the 1940s, Gloria Shepperson was the first documented colored operator hired in N.J. Bell System—most likely in the entire Bell System. Shepperson had to bring an anti-discrimination legal case to win her job as an operator (helped by the 1941 Fair Employment Practices Executive Order 8802 banning discrimination in hiring). Shepperson became C.W.A.'s Director of Ethnic Affairs and, in 1977, served as Assistant to C.W.A.'s Secretary-Treasurer Louis B. Knecht.

L.E.'s efforts were affecting a change in the battle at last. Nevertheless, he dared to believe victory lurked just around the corner.

In summer 1963, Southwestern Bell/AT&T finally conceded to union demands and allowed colored employees to bid on craft jobs. L.E., the C.W.A. #6131, and colored Southwestern Bell/AT&T employees had won. The company would soon integrate with Texas, and if it went well, then progression throughout the rest of the district would follow. The company would also list these craft positions as available for new applicants.

A few weeks later, L.E. received calls about jobs available in Victoria, Texas, and elsewhere. However, a problem arose: Nobody showed interest in leaving San Antonio for the small racist towns; therefore, blacks did not advance into craft positions. Nevertheless, the C.W.A. representative, Harper Nations, and Albert Bowles kept in touch. More communication from union heads was another positive sign that equal job opportunities for blacks would happen permanently. But unfortunately, no union employees wanted to take the chance or have an incident on their records.

L.E. had made big waves and mailed copies of union correspondences from R.F.K., and M.L.K. appeared to make a huge difference. The local support L.E. acquired also made a difference. If the AT&T C.W.A. president, who always spoke of fair labor practices and equality in employment, continued to hamper union demands for people of color, it would not reflect kindly on him. Now, Beirne's position was at risk. Mr. Glenn Watts assured L.E. that he would continue to support and a breakthrough was near.

In the meantime,

In San Antonio, members of the NAACP would repeat the march. Not a commemorative protest with no skin in the game, but an active movement during a time of risk. The march on Washington was for jobs and freedoms they still had to win. During the civil rights movement's height in the fight against non-discriminatory opportunities with major corporations, San

Antonio's demonstration during the civil rights movement was a battle for unbiased employment of sleeping car porters, the janitors at Southwestern Bell/AT&T, restaurant workers, and newspaper employees.

The San Antonio march organizers included the NAACP members L.E. Bennett, Dr. Bellinger, Rev. Black, Mr. Coleman, C.O.R.E. (Congress of Racial Equality), and the local Southern Christian Leadership Conference (S.C.L.C.). This group wanted people to awaken to the plight waged on their behalf—people of color on the east and west sides of

San Antonio. Demonstrators would hold up signs listing the companies against whom they were campaigning.

Seen by many as militant local rabble-rousers, the union officers and his NAACP cohorts were pushing the right buttons. They had been active in writing, making phone calls, and meeting with other area businesses about integrating their workforce. And finally, the walls were beginning to crack; L.E. knew the time was now for non-white Americans to elevate. Since the Executive Order, even the most prejudiced companies couldn't deny upward movement for minority employees.

By mid-August 1963, L.E. worked out of the Diamond Central Office and acquired another car, an old 1949 black Dodge four-door. L.E. drove the old Dodge, and Essie drove the Ford Fairlane. You could hardly pry her hands off the steering wheel. She ran errands whenever needed without worrying about coordinating days with L.E.

The family also purchased a more spacious new brick home with a fenced yard on Monterey Street, on the city's west side. Though in an all-black community, the house was closer to St. Mary's University, where L.E. continued his education, and the State Hospital, where Essie worked part-time. This affordable new home community started at $10,000. Essie loved the new address, which had three bedrooms, one bath, one carport, and hardwood floors. Hardwood floors were commonplace during this time.

L.E. didn't attend the March on Washington, but he watched Dr. King's historic "I Have a Dream" speech on television at work. Listening, he became so jubilant that he could hardly contain himself. Likened to a drink of premium pink champagne, a powerful tonic, this man vocalized all America's people of color's hopes and dreams, and the speech laid the groundwork for the Civil Rights Act of 1964.

Despite the national groundswell, L.E. still encountered people who attempted to block him. But every chance he got, he stood up and spoke his piece. L.E. was still standing up for the underdog.

M.L.K.'s words still echoed in his ears; L.E. left the office at the end of his shift. He was ecstatic, stirred, passionate, and on fire. He'd speak to members about repeating a similar march in San Antonio. When he arrived home, his next-door neighbor on Monterey Street, Carl Tyson, worked in the yard. The two men talked over the chain-linked fence about the miracle of Dr. King's speech for quite a while. They spoke about how he had stood there, King, forcefully conveying all they dreamed. Oh, they were proud of that brother.

Over dinner at home, the conversation about "I Have a Dream" continued. L.E. and Essie encouraged their children to participate in table discussions. They believed it enlightened the children and made them brighter, healthier, and more successful adults.

The company wasn't giving any clues about how and when to implement these changes. Management said someone was eligible for the promotion if they were in positive standing in their current position. Thus far, either no one had qualified or didn't want the job offer with the inconvenience of moving.

L.E. felt the company would do the basics to maintain credibility with the unions and the government. Then, when the time came to move a minority to a craft job, the company could claim they had kept their end of the bargain and heeded the presidential order that required equal opportunity employment. L.E. was doing canvassing of the members in all areas himself.

No one was interested in tokenism; union #6131 wanted genuine equal opportunity for all eligible employees. The company wanted to protect its position with all of the local unions. That required a continuous, relentless effort—more than one individual. It fit part of the bigger picture of getting better jobs and paying for non-whites all over America.

Beckon Of Light

They were not there when your brow was heavy with stress
When you contemplated which action to take, a
better way for us you wanted to make
How dare they over-rehearse
Their lines of disdain, in this, your hour of pain

Yes, made by God's Holy Hand,
you are yet a man
For there's only one that was perfect, did He send
For all the years you suffered and strived to take away
Yet they contrive, and down their noses lay

Look to the beckon of family,

your light they've always been;
look to our Lord and Savior
as he looked at his Father back then.

Time will be hard and slow,
But just keep looking into that beckon of light,
Because in it, God's mercy always flows.

By: Sharon Bennett, 2019
(Inspired after seeing Rev. Jesse Jackson on TV)

Muehlebach
Elevators and
Mailbox >>>

Muehlebach
Convention
/Ballroom

Regent Theatre

Back staircase

MUEHLEBACH

CWA Union Officers/Members

Joseph A. Beirne, president of the Communications Workers of America and a member of the 36-man AFL-CIO Executive Board

JOSEPH A. BEIRNE

Joseph Beirne,
CWA Union
President

**Joseph A. Beirne, CWA Union^>>
Photo and Union Meetings in
Colorado**

Glenn Watts II

**<<<Glenn E. Watts
late teen years**

**(L) Glenn E. Watts below in varied CWA Union Photos.
All photos usage approved by CWA Director of Communications of union
members/union business. [I do not own copyright to these photos.]**

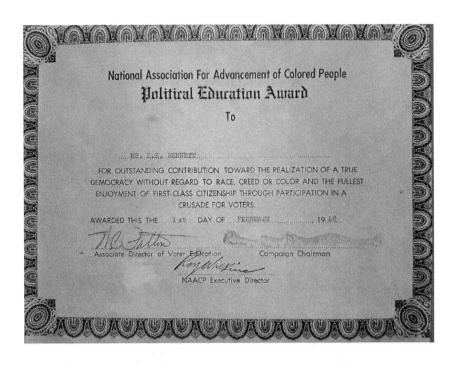

National Association For Advancement of Colored People

Political Education Award

To

......MR. L.E. BENNETT......

FOR OUTSTANDING CONTRIBUTION TOWARD THE REALIZATION OF A TRUE DEMOCRACY WITHOUT REGARD TO RACE, CREED OR COLOR AND THE FULLEST ENJOYMENT OF FIRST-CLASS CITIZENSHIP THROUGH PARTICIPATION IN A CRUSADE FOR VOTERS.

AWARDED THIS THE ....1st.. DAY OF ...FEBRUARY............, 19.68..

Associate Director of Voter Education   Campaign Chairman

NAACP Executive Director

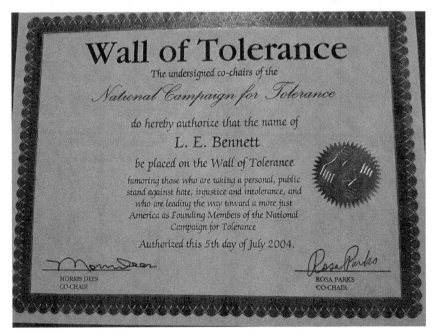

Wall of Tolerance

The undersigned co-chairs of the

National Campaign for Tolerance

do hereby authorize that the name of

L. E. Bennett

be placed on the Wall of Tolerance

honoring those who are taking a personal, public stand against hate, injustice and intolerance, and who are leading the way toward a more just America as Founding Members of the National Campaign for Tolerance

Authorized this 5th day of July 2004.

MORRIS DEES
CO-CHAIR

ROSA PARKS
CO-CHAIR

Albert Bowles (Left)

"Everyone should enjoy the same treatment, whether he lives in Laredo or Nueva Laredo (Mexico)." CWA Representative Albert S. Bowles (left) greets Mexican Consul Mario Romero Lopetegi on the picket line at Texas Hat Company in April of 1967. Whether it's working with ver.di in Germany to fight for the fair treatment of T-Mobile workers or Contraf-CUT in Brazil to fight for bank workers, CWA is proud to join international partners to fight against double standards.

Bell South Operators (L); Telephone Lineman (R)

Name placed on Wall of Tolerance Museum in his honor

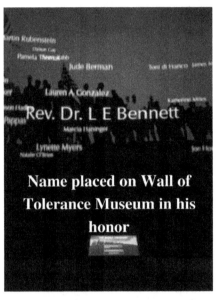

West side revitalization efforts

L.E. singing, "You are so beautiful," at Sharon's wedding

Galilee Miss. Bapt. Church

Rev. Dr. L.E. and Sis. Bennett in 2009

Sermons always ending with L.E. singing, a treat.

16

The Country Mourns

The country was progressing through August, and the glowing speech by Dr. King still rang in people's ears, the words carried on the wings of great feelings of happiness and possibilities.

It was late fall, and L.E. still worked at the Diamond Central Office. Friday, November 22, 1963, was a day he would never forget. It burned brightly in his mind. Probably no American would ever forget that date. The United States' young President stopped in San Antonio to pick up L.B.J. and headed to Carswell Airforce Base outside Dallas for a famous speech. The same as they had done in 1960.

Many were looking forward to watching his speech on television. Numerous social justice groups had gathered at the airport to voice disapproval on both sides of the political issues. Not able to attend due to work, L.E. had to watch in the breakroom and await reports from group members. But, as per Kennedy's usual, it was an excellent delivery.

That afternoon, L.E. and Melvin Porter returned to the office following lunch. L.E. went to the second floor to check the building conditions. He saw men sitting silently in their test positions, and women with tear-stained faces entered. Walter Cronkite was broadcasting live from CBS News Studios, taking his glasses off and choking back a sob as he announced that J.F.K. was dead.

L.E.'s body fell numb. Tears formed in his eyes, and he headed outside to walk around for a while. *Why would someone want to kill J.F.K.?*

L.E. kept saying to himself, "*The President is dead. The President is dead."* Finally, reality soon set in, and he knew that the man he respected and admired—an ally in his quest for equality—was genuinely dead.

What would this mean to the ongoing crusade in the country? AT&T? Would this make his job more difficult in bringing about equal employment? Would there be more assassinations? Medgar Evers was gunned down as well.

L.E. thought about M.L.K., and J.F.K.'s defiant words loudly spoke about equal rights and bravery to possess an audacious goal.

All weekend L.E. couldn't focus on his union work, glued to the TV as information developed around the assassination. He couldn't remember what the pastor preached Sunday, as he and the family had sat in the pew. Then, he got back into the car after services and listened to the radio to catch up on the news. His entire family shared L.E.'s melancholy. J.F.K. was dead, and the future appeared bleak.

The country had to move on, L.E. knew, but he sensed a nagging thought of apprehension about L.B.J.'s swearing-in as the next President. What could minorities expect in civil rights legislation from President Johnson?

The Constitution is a magnificent document. Would Johnson honor what J.F.K. had started? How strong would he stand behind the growing civil rights effort? L.B.J. was a U.S. senator from Texas, but L.E. wasn't current on Johnson's exact civil rights position. In Texas, many folks considered L.B.J. racist or mentally ill by a few people. L.E. wasn't sure which. Time would tell just how effectively Johnson implemented civil rights laws, built on JFK's legacy, and brought about changes to benefit people of color.

News reports continued to roll in on the assassination of J.F.K. by Lee Harvey Oswald and Oswald's killing by Jack Ruby. For L.E. and countless others, the pain of losing an advocate in such a high place was profound. Yet, the country loved J.F.K., his wife, Jackie, and the children. During the funeral procession, L.E. was especially touched by little John-John saluting the cortege as it passed in review.

It reminded him of standing by the bed where his father laid. L.E. had pulled back the white sheet to look upon the strong handsome face of his deceased father. He was not much older than John-John when Dan had died.

It was hard for L.E. to hold back the tears as he watched the ceremony. He commiserated with that little boy and recalled how life was growing up without his father. Would Jacqueline Kennedy be as supportive a mother to John-John as Anice Bennett had been to him? Of course, but in actuality, Jacqueline proved to be an excellent mother who continued with grace and dignity.

We Shall Pay Any Price

"We shall pay any price, bear any burden, meet any hardship, support any friend, oppose any foe to assure the survival and success of liberty."

President John F. Kennedy
January 20, 1961
(part of multiple printings from the Inaugural address)

17

Put Up or Shut Up

The union realized its aspirations in the winter of 1963. They were still working at the Diamond Central Office when Harper Nations, the Division Plant Personnel Supervisor, L.E., asked to meet with him for lunch. Harper Nations suggested the San Antonio International Airport.

Amidst the meal, Harper said, "L.E., we have two craft positions available in Corpus Christi for two linemen. They have a possible candidate for one of the positions with one condition. But the company's yet to find someone for the other position. Hence, I want to remind you of your previous statement."

L.E. stopped eating and stared at Nations, nervous about precisely what Nations referenced.

"Do you mean if you can't find anybody to fill a position, then as a last resort, I will go? To ensure a black union member gets the opportunity?"

Harper snapped his fingers and pointed at L.E.

"I remember very well," L.E. stated, then asked who the other man was considering agreeing to the position.

"L.E., now, it is put up or shut-up time. You have folks in high places rooting for you, like Watts. They've worked hard the past year to ensure change happens."

With his right arm bent and resting his face, L.E. asked, "Well, it's wonderful to know others have worked for us."

"Yes. I don't have to tell you that accepting this position will place you ahead of the other civil rights movement timelines for integration."

"Harper, have you exhausted the whole list of applicants? Everyone, I have typed letters requesting consideration for craft jobs?"

"Yes, I assure you I did," Nations insisted. "Charleston said he'd consider the offer, but he'll let me know; it sounds like a no to me. There's one possibility."

"Well, that's something. Who is it," L.E. asked.

"The other candidate is Lawrence Randle, your group treasurer. He'll go if you go. Albert Bowles and I are pulling for you, and a few local bigwigs have been voicing support. We know you and Randle will do the company proud."

"Wow, that's awesome. Lawrence is a dependable man and dear friend," exclaimed L.E. "But after all the work we've done, nobody else is ready to move?"

"It seems like no one else wants to go. Randle is the only one who may accept. I'll have to get someone outside the union if you cannot go. We will have to fill the position by other means. Furthermore, I don't have to tell you that the company's upper management and the C.W.A. president will think you are just making noise."

L.E. shook his head and let out a loud sigh. He was buried in union work and school, coordinating plans for the Houston telephone operators, helping plan a city march for solidarity and targeting equality for the following spring. Their local version of last summer's March on Washington.

Moreover, Nations explained, "The job would be two to three years, and the men are by May 1964."

L.E.'s eyes widened, and his mouth dropped. "God! So soon?" he gasped.

"I'm afraid so, L.E."

"Man, you're killing me. They're just trying to get rid of me," L.E. asserted.

"Well, you have been a thorn in their side, but, no. You've been convincing them, and times are changing. We want to be ahead of the curve. Besides, they don't want to have their hands forced. Furthermore, being a 'Do the Right Thing' pain in their ass, you're an excellent choice." Nations smiled.

L.E. rolled his eyes. "Yeah, right. Let me talk to Essie. Then, I'll get back to you."

"All right. Don't wait too long."

The gentlemen completed their lunch as Nations filled in L.E. about the new position and the city. He returned L.E. to the office shortly after their meal.

Once back at work, L.E. contacted James Charleston to inquire if he was seriously interested and if L.E. could give the union a decision. Regrettably, Charleston admitted too many things stood in his way and wouldn't take the position.

L.E. called Lawrence Randle to learn his status and understood he fully intended to go to Corpus Christi with his wife and six children. First, though, he would go only on one condition, L.E. must go with him.

Mr. Randle stated, "L.E. was energetic, straightforward, and honest, and those peckerwoods wouldn't break them. So instead, the two men together were going to break the peckerwoods."

L.E. continued calling union members, seeking someone to take this job opportunity. Unfortunately, the two Mexican union members hadn't ascended by that time. If L.E. couldn't find anyone, he would have to drop out of St. Mary's University and relocate to prevent the job from going to a non-minority and non-union person. Also, so Randle would not be alone.

His efforts to locate someone else were unsuccessful. But L.E. kept searching. After all, San Antonio was his family's home. L.E. and Essie Lee had only been in their brand-new home for more than a year. Plus, he had commitments with the NAACP for other local integration projects. But L.E. couldn't tolerate someone believing looking out for number one was his desire. So he tried diligently to get another person to accept the position. Yet, regardless of the time he'd spent writing letters for co-workers looking to rise through the ranks, no one was interested in going to Corpus Christi. They didn't want to face a wave of anger or a hostile work environment. They didn't want to sacrifice their current level of comfort.

After an exhaustive and relentless search, L.E. concluded he would have to be a man of his word and take the position, which meant massive changes. He'd have to leave the university, sell their home, and uproot his wife and children from familiar surroundings and friends.

L.E.'s statement had come back to bite him. He remembered his mother telling him about the type of man Dan Bennett had been. Dan always kept his word. And like his father, L.E. would stand behind his words, too.

He thought about the situation all the way home. How best to convince his spouse that he had to do what a man had to do? He needed Essie's support.

Try as he might, L.E. couldn't think of an excellent way to tell Essie. Her response would be of the utmost importance to him. Here was the woman the Lord had given him as his wife, and disappointing Essie was the last thing L.E. wanted to do. How would he make this seem plausible to her? What magic phrase could he dispatch?

As the car reached their home, L.E. had to face the music. At least, Essie liked Dorothy, Lawrence Randle's wife. Their relationship was one plus, but he saw no hope beyond.

The children were in the backyard playing. Essie met him at the door, and L.E. hugged and kissed her. L.E. took her hand and suggested they sit on the living room couch. He needed to tell her something.

L.E. unraveled the long and challenging story and that he pledged to take the job to ensure a minority filled the position.

Essie glared at him. Then she forced a small but brave smile and asked, "Daddy, can't you tell them you are joking and don't mean it?" (Essie called her husband Daddy to train the children—because they initially called him L.E.)

Essie lowered her head and sighed when he said backpedaling was not an option. She said things had been so hard, and she thought everything was downhill now. She paused and bit her nails as she turned away, and L.E. reached out to touch her knee. He worried about how his wife would respond. Essie directed her attention back to him and began to ask questions about Corpus Christi. About housing, schools, and family or friends in the area.

After they discussed all the angles about moving, Essie told L.E., "Daddy, I sure will hate leaving my home. But, honey, if this is what you must do, I think you already know I'm with you. Besides, I've never seen the ocean."

L.E. put his hand on his heart and released a loud gasp of relief. Those were the sweetest words he'd heard since the day he had asked Essie to marry him. He had only gotten this far because of his mother and Essie's vibrant and robust backing.

The day of the San Antonio march arrived. Union members made announcements to area residents, churches, and local newspapers. The gathering was at the corner of Iowa Street and New Braunfels at 9 a.m. in March 1964.

L.E. Bennett stood in solidarity with Dr. Ruth Bellinger, Eugene Coleman, Rev. Claude Black, other NAACP members, local ministers, family, and friends for the first civil rights march for employment equality in San Antonio. The committed group of approximately twenty-five to thirty people. Like M.L.K. advocated, the plan was to be a nonviolent event. Sorrowfully, no mainstream reporters covered this milestone. However, this trusted, politically active few and their families knew this march was the first political march in San Antonio for civil rights before M.L.K.'s death. They maintained a fight for impartiality when it wasn't accessible or easy to do so.

The city's east side was where most blacks lived, not downtown. Plus, it was difficult for the elderly to participate. They needed to see people determined to fight for them. So the group walked on the sidewalk along New Braunfels Street north towards the Army base.

The group talked amongst themselves and sang songs while holding up previously made signs. Residents on the adjacent streets waved as the demonstrators passed. The occasional car with white males passed and screamed obscenities from their windows. But it didn't deter the crowd. A few elders followed in their vehicles for protection. The procession finally reached the entrance to Fort Sam Houston Army Base. And soon, their task was complete.

The chapter planned to hold the march again in the summer and annually, except L.E. did not hear of a continuation after relocating to Corpus Christi for the phone company's craft position. After M.L.K.'s death, the mantle for an annual commemorative walk wouldn't be picked up until years later, in the mid-1980s, by L.E.'s first cousin, R.A. Callies. Because of R.A.'s efforts, San Antonio had one of the most massive commemorative marches in the nation.

May 1964 arrived before long for L.E. and Randle to report to Corpus Christi and their new boss, Glen Smith. Randle was more familiar with

Corpus because his father owned property. Randle loved staying with him on the coast to fish during summer. L.E.'s Aunt Gladys was the youngest sister of his mother, Anice. She was tall, firmly built, and brown-skinned, with glasses and a friendly, outgoing personality, who showed them around town. Sharon loved spending the night with Gladys and her husband, Uncle Percy.

L.E. and Randle shipped out first, and their families followed soon after. The company provided the men with temporary living arrangements at a motel on Shoreline Boulevard.

Meanwhile, job movement was happening in the San Antonio offices of AT&T. people of color were slowly moving into the craft jobs of installation and construction. The gate was open in the plant department. But the glass ceiling still had to be shattered in other departments, such as telephone operators and management. Mr. John Rucker, union vice president, and the NAACP focused on the battle, so L.E. was confident the effort would continue in his absence. However, he kept up regular phone contact.

Still, the first non-white telephone operators wouldn't arrive in Houston until late 1968. AT&T believed Houston would be a prime location to start the first colored operators due to its higher population of minorities. However, people weren't happy to hear about people of color's progression with a significant employer in some locales—coordination for San Antonio member support and inclusion at the Houston NAACP and CWA meetings.

L.E. notified the NAACP president, Dr. Boyd Hall, of the Corpus Christi area where he was relocating. Additionally, L.E. committed and continued to help with voter education and registration.

But L.E. attained a milestone. After nearly eight years of steady employment and acquiring civil rights for minorities in telecommunications at the main Southwestern Bell/AT&T offices, L.E. Bennett and Lawrence Randle became the first black linemen. So sweet was the taste of victory in L.E.'s mouth from climbing the mountain and making substantial gains.

After settling in over the weekend at the Corpus Christi motel, which overlooked the Gulf Coast, L.E. and Randle reported into work the following Monday morning. They were concurrently excited and nervous.

L.E. was concerned that his first day of work would mean being greeted by a sea of angry white faces.

The two new black linemen arrived early at 7:30 a.m. for their 8 a.m. shift. They met their construction foreman, Glen (Smitty) Smith, at the company storeroom on Caranchau Street. Glen was a straight arrow, not mean nor friendly but somewhat standoffish. The men eventually learned Smitty preferred to keep working and socializing separately. As Smitty introduced them to the men in the line gang, nobody seemed overly receptive to L.E. and Randle's arrival.

What else could they expect from the group? Indeed, not someone running out to greet them with a bear hug. But, the ice was broken, and like it or not, they would have to work together. They were each assigned a preceptor with whom they were to learn their duties. L.E.'s preceptor was George Treff, and Randle was appointed to work with Eddie. The preceptors told Bennett and Randle to dig trenches for the others.

Glen Smith was a slender, bespectacled man in his mid-to-late fifties. He often referred to any underling as a laddie. Competent in his job, Glen was emphatic about everyone learning theirs. He told the men he wanted results, not excuses.

Supervisor Smitty never gave the impression that he cared more about one Laddie than another. On the contrary, he expected the experienced men to show the greenhorns what it meant to be in a line gang. Alternatively, L.E. and Randle were assigned the worst tasks—chores so bad even their white counterparts called it slave labor. The co-workers were visibly relieved they no longer had to do these arduous tasks.

As weeks passed, L.E. and Randle were no longer the new guys. Treff was condescending and vile. While days existed when L.E.'s co-workers got on his nerves, it became a routine job—and like everyone else, he and Randle left the storeroom at the close of the day, dragging their butts on the ground from the sheer exhaustion of the day.

After work, L.E. and Randle discussed their day and the discrimination they'd experienced. Then, they brainstormed on possible resolutions to handle the conflicts while going to dinner. One of the options the men considered was to strangle their preceptors and leave their bodies in those same trenches they'd dug.

L.E. and Randle went by Mom's Café, a distant relative of L.E.'s owned the eatery. Mom was a sweet and endearing lady who served delicious soul food that represented the closest thing to home cooking. She fixed them dinner and faithfully prepared their lunch for the next workday.

A loud bang rang out on Sunday when L.E. and Randle were having dinner at Mom's restaurant. After the shot, police sirens whined, tires screeched, and an ambulance arrived. The door thrust open, and a man ran into the café and sat at a table. Panting, he began talking about killing someone because a man had tried to take his money, which couldn't be allowed. There was going to be trouble, so, awkwardly, L.E. and Randle quietly rose and got out in a hurry. L.E. prayed for his family's safety and wished he could attend church. This incident at the café and not having his family in Corpus Christi troubled him.

L.E. quickly realized the problems with his preceptor continued despite his resolution interventions. Finally, L.E. reached the boiling point where the sight of Treff made him sick to his stomach. Treff spoke disrespectfully to L.E., hovering over him like a vulture, inspecting and peering at every detail, not letting up as the months elapsed—or L.E. got better at his lineman job. Finally, the company hired Mexican-American union members into craft-level positions via open bids in Corpus and other areas.

L.E. finally resolved that he couldn't let Treff dog him or upset him. Mistreating others gave this person joy; however, a whole generation of black people whose futures depended on the success or failure of L.E. Bennett. If he failed, it could set back the integration. So he needed to do what he did and simplify it!

Despite how L.E. grew to feel about Treff, the man was doing his job, and he was knowledgeable. So L.E. decided to take a negative and turn the situation into a positive one. Although Treff's attitude was pugnacious and nasty at times, he was still a damn excellent lineman. So L.E. pledged to learn everything about being a top lineman. As a result, whenever George Treff came behind him to check on his work, L.E. didn't react badly or take the review personally.

After several months in Corpus Christi, L.E. rented a home for the family, who arrived soon after. Wretchedly, the residence was bug-infested and unacceptable for Essie. She quickly found them something more suitable, a 1,100-square-foot white house built around the 1800s, at 2509

Koepke Street, right across from Crossley Elementary School. The home's north-of-town location proves to be convenient for the children. It was a standard old house with beautiful hardwood floors, three bedrooms, two bathrooms, a detached garage, missing roof tiles, and needing repairs. Essie loved the neighborhood.

The next-door neighbors were Felmon and Bertha Barnes, sterling people with their children. Their daughter Jackie and Sharon became friends; Michael, Glenn, and Carlise also befriended the Bennett children.

A small old grocery store with creaky, thick wood floors was on the corner. Significant glass cases sat at one end of the counter that held meat. Essie never shopped there. However, the children bought candy with their allowance.

The home was in a racially mixed neighborhood of lower-middle-class people, close to Aunt Gladys, Anice's sister. L.E. and Essie depended on them for help. First, Gladys and her husband, Percy, took the family out for fun. Then, they all caught fish for dinner while driving the boat in the ocean.

Essie went to Crossley to register the children for the 1964–1965 school year. However, the principal told Essie she had to go to the Negro school in the Cuts on the east side and get their admission packets. Offended, Essie explained that she already had the children's transfer packets from San Antonio, and her kids never attended a Negro school in the Cuts. So, to register them, Essie had to acquire transfer forms from the Negro school.

L.E. was ahead of the south with the integration goals for AT&T, and he wanted his children to be ahead. He wanted corporations to invest in black and Hispanic neighborhoods, have job opportunities in low-income communities, pay fair wages, eliminate redlining, and equally advance minorities in the company—and he wanted them to be safe.

Essie found work at Spohn Hospital as a nurse's aide in the nursery to bring in extra income. She took the nighttime shift from 11 p.m. to 7 a.m. The new family routine meant L.E. had to fix Sharon's hair for school mornings. He wasn't good at it, but he did his best. Sharon soon learned how to do her hair quickly, or Essie did it three nights before leaving for work. Longingly, Sharon missed the French-braided angel rings her mother had put on the top of her head. But Essie made up for it by doing the angel ring on her off-nights.

However, working nights was extremely difficult for Essie, especially when she couldn't get eight hours of sleep. But the sacrifice was worth it for her family, and she kept going. The home had a front and back door that stuck and creaked. The noise alerted her when the children tried to exit the house once they were home from school. Essie took the job because she discovered the sitter abused Kenneth after being sick and having diarrhea. The sitter locked Louis and Sharon out of the house and whipped Kenneth's naked body mercilessly with switches from a backyard tree. The teen sitter didn't stop until Sharon yelled that she was going to the neighbors to call the police.

After the malicious event, Essie went to work at the Central Kitchen for the Corpus Independent School District. This job allowed her to earn income during the children's school hours. Essie worked there until ascertaining she was pregnant with their fourth child. During the middle of Essie's pregnancy, she went to work at Memorial Hospital.

The Bennetts traveled to Houston in March 1966 due to what doctors described as the unrelenting flu-like illness of L.E.'s brother Mack. However, they discovered Mack had cancer. His situation worsened steadily over the months.

Mack's homegoing service would take place in October 1966. During the trip back to Houston, Essie, Martha, Norcie, and Janie discovered they were expecting around the same time. Norcie birthed Darrell, Martha had Audrey, Janie (Floyd's 2nd wife) delivered Greta, and Essie had a big-eyed beautiful girl on January 14, 1967, whom L.E. named Lisa Elizabeth.

Lisa was a daddy's child from the start. As soon as she started to walk, she wanted to go everywhere L.E. went. There weren't seatbelts in the cars, so L.E. put her behind his shoulder as Lisa stood in the front seat. He could use his shoulder to keep her in the position. That way, whenever he made a quick stop, he could protect her. Lisa slept in a crib in the room with her parents until she was three. Afterward, she shared a room with Sharon.

Work remained like slave labor, L.E. thought. The pay was better than janitorial services, but it was still less than their white counterparts. L.E. and Randle had used to work inside air-conditioned buildings. Now, they were working outside in the hot, humid weather. It was back-breaking work, and each day presented many new challenges.

The work was dirty and brutal. But it was also gratifying because L.E.

and Randle learned something new each day and could see the fruits of their labor. By evening, they had something new to discuss. Some days the preceptors had high praise for them, calming their anger.

But make no mistake, there were other days when L.E. and Randle wanted to kill somebody. However, they understood the duties and responsibilities of serving as the first black linemen in Corpus Christi for AT&T/Bell Systems. They were there to work, to be as successful as possible. Because when they finished the dirty work, there would be something better up the road—a job advancement that meant fellow minorities could also have the chance to move up.

By this time, L.E. had graduated from working with George Treff and was assigned to a truck to perform jobs unsupervised. Between 1964 and 1967, L.E. went through many job assignments, and the pressure was immense. Each was a step up. He still drank Pepto-Bismol-like water. While he was a lineman, he bid on a cable splicer job.

One day, Glen Smith unexpectedly visited him on the job site. Smitty walked up to the base of the pole where L.E. was working and hollered up, "Laddie, come down. I need to talk with you."

L.E. secured his equipment and began his descent. Once L.E. reached the bottom of the pole, Smitty was already back in his vehicle. L.E. walked over and sat in the truck. Smitty had excellent news: The company had accepted L.E.'s bid for the cable splicer position. He gave L.E. the particulars on reporting to his new job assignment.

L.E. thanked his old boss, adding, "Maybe, I might have an occasion to work for you again. Who knows."

Smitty looked at him seriously and responded, "No, laddie, you won't ever be working for me again. But, if anything, I may wind up working for you one day. You're the first black cable splicer, and when you leave here, I know that you are going onward and upward. I wish you the best."

With that, Smitty shook L.E.'s hand and thanked him for a well-performed job, then he departed, leaving L.E. with his mouth gaped open in surprise. At the base of the pole, L.E. reminisced about his journey. Being a lineman was no small achievement. But both he and Randle had exceeded supervisor expectations. Randle accepted a job bid and relocated his family back to San Antonio. His request was a step down from lineman, but Randle would be inside and making advancements from that strategic position.

L.E. was to report to Ed Janota, his new foreman in the cable splicing crew. Ed had become a foreman not long ago, himself. They assigned L.E. to Richard Trujillo, his preceptor, who had a superb ability as a craftsman. They soon shared a strong friendship. Both Janota and Trujillo worked for the company for a long time. When the opportunity had come for non-whites to apply for craft jobs, these men quickly applied for those outside positions, trained, and achieved advancement as foremen in Corpus, which had a higher Latin employee population.

The two men worked laying the telephone cable along Padre Island Drive, and Janota was determined to meet his deadlines. When L.E. and Richard worked in a utility hole, Janota showed up one night. He told L.E. and Richard they could be working a little faster. The discussion led to a brief verbal altercation, as the splicers defended the quality of their job performance. Janota commented on how he identified who L.E. was and had achieved advancement independently, and no Negro from San Antonio had helped him. L.E. was flabbergasted by the comments. Janota hadn't gained any advance until after Bell agreed to C.W.A. union demands, according to the records. L.E. didn't care and went on with his work.

Cable splicing was reputable work, and L.E. enjoyed the new job experience. Things were going quite well heading into the winter. L.E. soaked up everything, and he learned quickly. His objective was to immerse himself in aspects of each position because there were plans to rise in the ranks. In addition, knowing each work level would allow him to comprehend what other workers endured. L.E.'s goal was from the street to the division management offices he planned to be in one day.

One day, L.E. was cutting in a new telephone terminal off Padre Island Drive, close to the Wyman electronic switching system office. This terminal would provide operation for many new work and home phone numbers. It was freezing that day. L.E. erected his tent for protection from the intense cold, but the winds blew underneath the tent. L.E.'s hands were so near freezing that he could hardly splice the cable pairs. He had a nice thick mustache mixture of ice and snot.

When L.E. decided this reputable work was for the birds, he knew there had to be a better way to earn a living, so he resolved to lobby for an inside job. L.E. placed a request for a Central Office frame job and was accepted. The frame job meant managing the leading network of electronic line connections for telephone calls.

L.E. worked under Jim Gilbert's supervision at the Terminal Office. Jerry Darden, Ernest Camiel, and Robert Gunnels were his other co-workers, and the men's chemistry was terrific. Next, Gilbert sent L.E. to the Wyman Office, an Electronic Switching System (E.S.S.). There, a man by the name of Green taught L.E. the ropes. He then had a broader skillset regarding telephone circuitry in two offices.

In late September 1967, Hurricane Beulah ripped through Corpus and caused much damage. The work required cleaning the city up and having telephone lines repaired. The switching office was also a disaster shelter, so the Bennett family went there when the hurricane hit Corpus Christi. The basement floor had cots; families received dinner bags of Church's Chicken. L.E. showed the children his area as he walked around doing work on the switches. The kids loved watching their daddy do his job.

The Struggle

He fought in the battle
for the cause of civil rights.
God is good all the time!
The struggle was nearing an end.
Winning the battle to elevate minorities in the workplace was near.
But the spiritual struggle was still there.
It began to take dominance in his life.

Sharon Bennett 1999

18

The Spelling Bee

With her arms tightly around her mother, screaming and crying, Sharon yelled, "He said I couldn't be in the Crossley Spelling Bee because I'm a Negro."

L.E. Bennett had four children, and Sharon was the second born of two boys and two girls. She was a thin tomboy, with long black hair worn in two ponytails and bangs or a French braid circling her head. L.E. was heavy into the fight for civil rights and equality in employment and climbing the ladder when he came home to hysteria. But, alas, things for all people weren't changing fast enough.

One late fall day in 1967, Sharon cried when she came home from school. She was ten years old and in the fourth grade at Crossley Elementary. Sharon had been excited all summer and planned to participate in the school's spelling bee. Instead, she studied the family encyclopedias and dictionaries and read over one-hundred books over the summer. The program gave students a state decal for every book they had read. Upon completing the U.S. map, the student may start another.

The school held the competition one day a week in mid-fall. The chosen in-school moderator gave the word to the standing student. If a student got the correct answer, they stayed in the program. If the student didn't respond correctly, they were out of the program.

The in-school spelling program continued until the only two left were Sharon and her opponent, a white female who wore glasses and had shoulder-length blonde to light straight brown hair. The moderator gave the word to the little blonde girl, who didn't spell it correctly. The next word went to Sharon, who took her time before spelling correctly; finally, the teacher took a deep breath and turned to the principal. The principal of the school nodded back.

Taking a deep breath, the woman turned back to the student and said, "Yes, Sharon, correct. You've won and are our school representative for the citywide competition!"

Sharon was delighted and couldn't wait till school was out to run home to tell her parents.

The school bell rang, and Sharon waited for her brothers to go home together in front of the school. When her siblings arrived, she hopped and skipped across the street to their home.

Her mother, Essie, was in the kitchen preparing food for them. Essie was thrilled by the news and started planning her little girl's outfit and hairstyle. Sharon was asleep when L.E. arrived home, but Essie told him the fantastic news. They were both so proud and talked about their hopes and dreams for their children until they fell asleep.

The following day the young Bennett siblings ate breakfast and crossed Koepke street to school; Sharon hummed a happy tune with a pep until she arrived home.

School started in the usual manner with the pledge of allegiance, morning prayer, and announcements. Afterward, the teacher checked the roll and announced to everyone that their classmate had won the school's spelling bee. Next, she asked Sharon to step forward and placed a brightly colored ribbon on the shoulder of her dress. Most of the class erupted in clapping.

Sharon couldn't help grinning ear to ear and proudly saying, "Thank you."

There was a knock at the classroom door. A male student entered to hand the teacher a message, and with his head lowered, he quickly left.

The teacher read the note, stopped smiling, and exhaled sharply. "Sharon, the principal wants you in his office, please."

"Okay," she said.

Her heels clicked as she walked the long polished white hallway to the administration offices. A white woman at the administration desk said nothing, only pointed to the principal's office, smirking. Sharon knocked on the open door, and the principal waved her in. Sharon strolled into the office, and the principal aimed at an oversized wooden chair directly in front of his desk.

"Take a seat, Ms. Bennett," Mr. H. said.

Sharon sat in the wooden chair, her feet dangling.

"Sharon, Crossley Elementary is extremely proud of you for being so smart and winning the Crossley Spelling Bee. We'd love to have one of our students make it to the National Spelling Bee in Washington, D.C."

"Thank you," Sharon smiled as she gazed proudly at her ribbon and began to swing her legs joyfully.

The principal stood, walked to the front directly across from Sharon, removed his glasses, and leaned back on his desk. "But, we can't let you participate in the citywide competition."

A look of concern replaced her smile. "But why?"

"Well, to be honest, it's because you're a Negro. The city won't let a Negro student compete."

"What?" Sharon whimpered.

"Let's not make this any harder than it is, young lady. You can go back to class now," he said, pointing at the door.

Sharon stood and approached the principal's door, lowering her head, pulled the ribbon off her dress, and dropped it into his wastebasket. She cried, walking back down those polished white floors through those long halls of white walls. Stopping outside the classroom, the child wiped her wet face and dried those small hands on her dress before entering. Sharon walked straight to her desk as the teacher told her what page of the lesson the class was on; she opened the book. Sharon cried during the day, but the teacher never asked what was wrong or helped.

Finally, the school bell rang, and the children headed home. The Bennett boys were horsing around, but Sharon remained quiet as they crossed the street. Upon reaching their front porch, she ran into the house and straight to her mother in the kitchen, who was preparing their snack before starting dinner. Sharon tightly grabbed her mother around the hips and cried so loudly. Essie was startled as she pried the child's arms away. Then, she knelt to clasp the face, moving her child back. The boys froze in place with their mouths open.

"Baby? Baby? Oh, my God! Please, tell me what's the matter. Did someone hurt you?" Essie asked. At the same time, glancing over Sharon's body.

"They won't let me do the spelling bee cuz I'm a Negro," she stammered.

"Oh, no. Oh, no," Essie exclaimed. She held her daughter tightly. "I'm so sorry that happened, sweetie. Mommy's so sorry," Essie cried.

"How can they say no? I had spelled all the words right, Mommy, I always get A's."

Eventually, calming Sharon, Essie could get her to eat a snack, start her homework, and play. L.E. couldn't get home fast enough for Essie. L.E. arrived within an hour. Greeting L.E. at the door, Essie kissed him solemnly and asked him to their bedroom for a serious conversation. It was their way to get privacy and never disagree in front of the children.

This time, Essie didn't call the kids to eat right away. Of course, Essie wasn't the curser, but the day would be a record for both of them.

"Something terrible happened to our daughter today."

Confused and concerned, L.E. sternly asked, "What in the Hell do you mean, Essie? Somebody touched my girl?" He gestured outside their bedroom door.

Tears began to stream down Essie's face as she touched his arm. "The principal told her she couldn't be in the Citywide Spelling Bee because she's a Negro."

"Goddamn it! Those racist bastards. I will call the school first thing in the morning and see if I can help them correct this shit. I'll call the school board, too, if I have to."

"I don't think it's going to help anything. I'm sure those folks have their minds made up. Besides, we don't want our children to become intended targets, Essie said."

"What in Hades am I supposed to do, Twinkie? Let it ride? I didn't want this bullshit to affect our children. I'm supposed to shield them from this. It's not right."

"It may not be right, Daddy. But it's our life. You are the expert here. You can't protect them from everything. Worry about your daughter's heart. Help her understand, heal, and get past this treacherous act."

"Help her?"

"Yes, help her." Essie touched him gently on his chest, left the room to prepare dinner plates, and called the children to wash up.

L.E. was enraged as he grunted, placed his hands on his hips, and stared down at his shoes while tapping his foot. He tried to calm himself as he went to wash up for dinner. L.E. mulled over what to say to his daughter. How could he get a ten-year-old to understand these injustices due to her skin color?

The atmosphere around the table was thick and quiet. Even though L.E. tried to involve the children in conversation, their responses were abrupt. Finally, the children excused themselves and began their evening routine after their meal. Sharon took her bath first and returned to Essie to get her hair brushed and styled.

Essie stood up after completing her hair. L.E. chose that moment to speak with her. He grabbed a chair from the end of the table and placed it in front of Sharon.

Sitting down and taking a deep breath, L.E. took Sharon's hands. "Moochie Baby," he said, using his pet name for her, "I hear you had a rough day. How are you doing?"

"Yes, Sir. I can't be in the spelling bee cuz I'm a Negro," she whined.

"Baby, Daddy is so sorry that happened to you. I want you to know you're as smart and capable as those other children."

"Then why can't I do it, Daddy? What's wrong with being a Negro?"

Touching his forehead to Sharon's and touching her chin, L.E. continued. "Nothing is wrong with it! Some people hate others just because they're different. Some feel they are better than everyone else, and people of color should be their servants. I want you to know that you are a beautiful, strong, and a smart young lady. You are more than enough and deserve anything for which you work. But colored people can do twice as much and be twice as good, and a racist will still think they are giving us something."

"That's not fair. I don't like that and want to do the spelling bee."

"I know. Life isn't fair, and you may not do this one thing. But, in your life, you'll do many other wonderful things. Okay?"

"Mm-hmm," Sharon murmured, with head lowered.

L.E. hugged Sharon and kissed her on the cheek while patting Essie on her shoulder and attempted to give a poorly executed smile as he turned to go shower. As L.E. went into their bedroom and closed the door, there was a loud thud.

The sound scared Essie, and she yelled, "Are you okay?"

"Yeah, I ran into the dresser," L.E. responded.

The evening continued with thoughts of his children and the conflicts they had or may experience in school. These thoughts caused anguish as L.E. strived to get some sleep. When Essie finally came to bed, he hugged and kissed her. L.E. thanked her for being a wonderful mother. Eventually, he fell asleep and rested, preparing for his upcoming workday with her in his arms.

On a few weekends, L.E. took the children to the T-heads, a marina, and a park with paved pathways on Shoreline Drive. L.E. loved to catch rays, watch how the sun glistened off the ocean, and listen to the sound of the waves as they rushed in. It had a relaxing, cleansing effect on him.

L.E. even took the children to an air show to see airplanes and witness the Thunderbirds perform tricks as they flew. The broadcaster announced that the Thunderbirds had left Austin and would be there in two minutes. The kids didn't believe it. Suddenly there was a rumbling sound, and their bodies vibrated. In two minutes flat, the jets flew overhead to give a show. The crowd laughed and clapped in amazement.

A few weeks after the Crossley Spelling Bee incident, L.E. took his kids to the "T-Heads" again. Kenneth rode on his skateboard, Louis played with his model airplanes and Sharon roller-skated.

Louis was a kindhearted and sweet child. He was most like his mother, Essie. Oddly, he wasn't the best student, but he was a master at understanding how airplane engines worked and drawing. Louis' drawings were intricate and precise. That was what he enjoyed doing—not hanging out at birthday parties or playing sports, and for that, he was thought strange by his classmates. For Louis to fight would take much poking the bear.

Sharon was generous, loyal, and thoughtful. Despite this, as a child, if anyone wronged her brothers or herself or pushed and didn't correct their behavior, she'd pound them. Sharon was most like L.E., and she would tell you about injustices.

Kenneth was bright, curious, and fast-moving; he loved to ride his bike and skateboard fast. Kenneth loved things a thrill a minute. His and Louis' discipline was due to mutual agitation and fighting. Louis usually didn't care, and that angered Kenneth.

The kids had their favorite treats, and L.E. and Essie tried to appease them. Louis liked the yellow cake, vanilla ice cream, orange soda, and Elvis Presley. Sharon loved strawberry shortcake, strawberry ice cream, red soda, and the Tempting Temptations, while Kenneth was wild about chocolate cake, chocolate ice cream, root beer soda, and James Brown. L.E. bought their first record albums of their favorite artists, and when the entertainers came to town, he took them to the concerts.

L.E. trusted that these outings allowed bonding time with his children and for him to relax. At the "T-heads," he watched as the kids played as if they didn't worry about the world. L.E. still hadn't forgotten about Sharon's spelling incident.

As she made another circle near L.E., he called Sharon over.

Smiling, he said, "Hey Moochie Baby, how have you been doing since the spelling tryouts?"

"Fine," she said, not looking at her father.

"Only fine?"

She turned away. "Yes, Sir. Fine."

"Well, listen, I have a great idea. Why don't you join a debate team? They have a class at the community center, which involves mastering words."

"I don't want to do that."

"Really? But you're sharp. You can be a lawyer one day or go into government."

"Hmph, I don't want to."

L.E. asked, "Well, what do you want?"

After a few moments, Sharon looked at her father and responded, "I wanted you to get me into that spelling bee. Help me like all the other people you've been helping. Why didn't you help me?"

L.E. winced as he focused down at the ground.

"Daddy, can I go back and skate?"

He waved his hand like shooing a fly. "Yeah, beat feet."

Sharon stopped after a few feet away and turned back to her father. Tears were welling up in his eyes as he offered a partial smile with one side of his lips going up. She provided a half-smile back, turned, and skated off. *He should have called the school,* he thought.

Although some all-white schools in Corpus Christi allowed integration between 1955 and 1962, discrimination still hovered over the city. However, after a class-action lawsuit, it was filed in 1968 by Jose Cisneros for the black and Hispanic steelworkers' organization for desegregations. The Corpus Christi Independent School District ordered the desegregation by the 1971–72 school year. The busing of over 15,000 students across town began after that.

L.E. kept in touch with Rucker and Nations, assisting with integration support. That day, he wondered how everyone felt about the fight for equality in San Antonio, so he called Dr. Bellinger of the NAACP and Mr. Eugene Coleman of SNAP News. They told him that progress with job reform was still slow and laborious, even with the Executive Order. They had hoped to be further along by then. Several folks accepted positions, yet many were still afraid. It was almost like they were losing ground.

Though better jobs for people of color were available, the offerings were usually jobs white people didn't even want or hostile work environments. Yet, L.E.'s allies were hopeful; they expected black telephone operators— including Jewish women—to integrate before the 1968s year's end. Also, L.E. identified with the hostile environment but was happy about the telephone operators because he had started that battle.

L.E. listened to Bellinger's planned speech for an important upcoming meeting. In her remarks, he gave Bellinger some tips on specifics to counteract the conference's arguments. Dr. Bellinger admitted that Rucker was a good man, but he didn't have the precision, zeal, or quick repartee that L.E. had. Rucker also preferred not to give the speech. Contrary, she begged L.E. to come back and assist them with this task in Houston.

L.E. agreed that he would be there for the next divisional meeting for the union on operators. They wished each other well and committed to speaking again soon. L.E. called Nations the following day and asked for assistance to attend this meeting without being considered absent from work. Nations advised that it wouldn't be a problem to assist him. Next, L.E. called Rucker to ensure he was okay with L.E. speaking. Rucker was relieved and thrilled with the option.

There always seemed to be a flurry of activity. Then, in June 1968, it had been four years since arriving in Corpus; the growing Bennett family purchased a home at 234 Westgate Drive, close to Miller High School and the Buccaneer Stadium. That was within walking distance, and the family attended many Miller Buccaneer football games.

Approximately 1,300 square feet, the home was a modest three-bedroom, two-bath with a separate dining and living room. The rooms had hardwoods, except for the carpeted living room. L.E. studied at the dining room table when he could.

Shortly after these Houston meetings, Southwestern Bell/AT&T agreed that women of color, including Jewish women, would begin employment and training before 1968 ended. Then, in December 1969, abducted, brutally stabbed, raped, and murdered, walking to work from the downtown company parking lot, was twenty-five-year-old Ms. Diane Maxwell Jackson, a telephone operator. A man found her body in an old shack behind an abandoned gas station. The murderer of Ms. Diane Maxwell Jackson was found over thirty years later due to FBI identification of latent prints from her stolen red Mustang. In 1969 that news report greatly saddened L.E. He wondered if it had anything to do with the unions' push to integrate the operators starting in Houston or a random act of violence (FBI Cold Case, 2008, Diane Maxwell Jackson).

Words Matter

We have ceased to be our brother's keeper.
We have abandoned our sisterly love.
The classes separate us.
The races divide us.

Politics intoxicate us.
We are confused by religions,
blinded by hatred.
The walls of our houses are thicker.

You cannot penetrate it.
There are solid and impenetrable.
Words do matter!

Unknown internet poet 2020

19

Internal Struggle

L.E. and Essie would try different jobs to earn extra income in Corpus Christi. First, they decided to work nights cleaning a bank building for a while, but that didn't pan out. Working day and night and extra work meant less time with the children.

In 1968–69, L.E. established a small business club and several other young men, including Sam Johnson, a local barber. Their goal was to start the business by renting space to sell department store–type merchandise. These men were like-minded and entrepreneurs. The market seemed ripe for this undertaking, but it didn't prosper. So the next plan was to open a nightclub on Greenwood Street. Black companies were in the "Cuts," and locals had complained that there was no place suitable to go except down on the Cuts. So the gentlemen looked at an area off Leopard Street close to Saint Matthew's Church and Mom's Café, near the Cuts. The Cuts was a deprived neighborhood of one- and two-story rundown buildings, with several nightclubs, gambling joints, liquor stores, and places to procure opposite sex's companionship if one so desired.

It was desolate during the day but came alive at night. One could get a good dose of black culture on the Cuts. It was where you wore the latest fashions and your best cologne. You could get all the action you were looking for, whether you wanted to shake your booty, have a funky good time, or enjoy home cooking of smothered steak with onions, rice, and gravy.

You went to the Cuts to hear a bar or club jukebox blaring with B.B.

King's "Sweet Sixteen" or the Temptations; "My Girl," or Sam Cooke's "I Was Born by The River."

If you were so inclined, you could do some gambling and raise a little Hell. But you also ran the risk of losing your life. You had to think fast and move twice as quickly, and if you stayed too long in one place, someone might have to call the undertaker.

To offer a safer alternative to the Cuts nightlife, L.E. and Essie opened a new club called "The Tropics." But the business started slowly. It wasn't what you call a barn burner.

Shortly after noon, L.E. was at The Tropics by himself, sitting at the bar on Saturday. In his early forties, a gentleman entered the front door and walked up to the bar, where L.E. was seated.

L.E. greeted him, and they made small talk. Then the man asked where he could find some gambling. L.E. said he didn't know but suspected that he'd find that activity in the Cuts. The gentleman then inquired as to where he could find a girl. Again, L.E. didn't know but recommended the Cuts.

Finally, the gentleman said, "You know; when I walked in here and looked at you, I could tell right away that this is not your place. Anyone in this type of business knows the answer to those questions. But you don't, because you don't care about those things. They are not of interest to you. So I want to give you some good advice. Go back to church, where you belong! This bar is not your type of business. You will never be happy doing this type of thing."

The gentleman bade L.E. a good day, got off the barstool, and made his way out.

L.E. knew the stranger was correct. His actual place was in church. Being anywhere else, L.E. felt like a fish out of water. He went home and told Essie about the encounter. Her eyes widened at the story. Shortly after, the Bennetts agreed to close The Tropics and return to what they knew best: serving the Lord.

During the family's years in Corpus Christi, they became involved in their new community and joined the St. Matthew Missionary Baptist Church, where Rev. Elliot Grant is the pastor. The experiences at the church were memorable for the family. L.E. was on the deacon board and sang in the male chorus; Essie was an usher. In addition, the boys and girls participated in the children's church. Except for the teacher, they loved the church, a skinny, middle-aged lady named Mrs. Fuquar. She was cock-eyed; one eye looking left and the other seeming right. Whenever she instructed the Sunday School class or disciplined a child verbally, they weren't supposed to laugh and did everything to hold the giggles inward.

L.E. helped with the accounting of the church. The pastor trusted and relied on him. St. Matthews didn't have an associate minister, and the pastor had to leave for a family emergency. The pastor asked L.E. to deliver Sunday's sermon. In their way, Rev. Grant, Rev. Langham, and Rev. Graham would all tell him that he had a calling to acknowledge. L.E. was terrified of the idea but did a great job. However, L.E. refused to stand behind the pulpit. L.E. was still running from the idea of being a minister. He stood on the main level in front of the congregation. However, this little gesture didn't force him to acknowledge the call. He eventually helped the pastor find an associate minister.

The church was constructing new low-income apartments financed by the federal government. L.E. served as chairman of the advisory committee for the project. Although he struggled in his new position as a cable splicer, he found a way to help his fellow man.

The committee worked closely with Mr. Harris, a government representative out of San Antonio. L.E. assisted with bringing the project through its formative stage of approved plans, including building permits and construction. L.E. looked forward to seeing its conclusion and ribbon-cutting, but he had received a promotion and relocation to San Antonio before completion. So he missed the happy occasion.

L.E. recalled a vision he had as a child. Perhaps a premonition. He was behind the house, down near the woods. He preached to the seamy beans when a chilling wind gripped him and held him motionless. He suddenly saw himself standing behind a pulpit, preaching to a large congregation. This frightened L.E. tremendously, and he ran back to the house. He sat down under the window, where Anice kept her sewing machine, to give his heart a chance to stop racing. His mother asked Baby—her pet name—if anything was wrong.

Still breathless from his scare, L.E. was reluctant to confess what he had seen.

He answered, "No, ma-a-am, I'm all right."

As customary, he and the family would spend time with relatives on some weekends, as long as L.E. wasn't traveling to provide NAACP voter registration engagement and projects or inquiry requests by fellow union members. Otherwise, you could find him relaxing with one of his siblings, other relatives, or with the children.

The time with family regenerated him and helped to relax his busy mind. But unfortunately, when the visit was over and the kids went to bed, his mind reverted to the difficulties of equal rights and strategies.

There was another battle that L.E. was fighting. The internal struggle of not wanting to accept the call to the ministry. Also, he had not fully grieved the loss of his mother. As far as L.E. was concerned, he was ministering when he helped people register to vote or enroll as NAACP members. If he prayed for guidance with civil rights, the call to minister would be more robust.

L.E. Bennett was raised as a Christian and practiced that faith in the church. There were family ministers and singers. But, he thought, *Am I not giving enough of myself by being a deacon, singer, and the church treasurer? What about the load I'm carrying with church projects and growth? My burden is massive, and I don't need another cross.*

Besides, dealing with church folk was another animal of its own. L.E. continued to have stomach pangs, and he drank Pepto-Bismol, took Tums, or mixed baking soda to ease the problem.

L.E. managed to stop smoking, but he picked up another habit. When it was just him and Green working out of the Terminal Office, parking was not a problem, and they took turns driving to coffee breaks. Since basic army training, L.E. had not drunk coffee, so he drank soda. On evenings out, he drank beer.

Soon, L.E. began to drink brown liquor when with his siblings on their family visits. Then, not long after, he drank when alone. If he could drown the internal voices guiding him to minister, everything would be alright.

After a trying day of work, civil rights meetings with his NAACP members, or a drive to one of the area towns to support Negro employees, L.E. drank his brown liquor, his silencer. He wouldn't think about his parents' untimely deaths or how much he missed them and longed for their presence. He wouldn't think about how unfair it was to be without his father. He wouldn't ponder how his brother Lloyd had been shot in the head and stomach like a dog three days before L.E.'s birthday and was no longer there. Instead, L.E. strived for them to be proud of him. Any education L.E. received or a blow he struck for equality was for them too.

Once L.E. arrived home, he stumbled into the kitchen to eat Essie's meal, kissed the sleeping kids, showered, and slept till dawn. The cycle repeated itself.

The liquor problem only appeared to solve stressors that a corporate ladder climber and a civil rights activist experienced. L.E.'s eloquent persuasion speech and strategies became lost on his children, especially the boys. He had no patience with them, and discipline was fast and harsh.

After much effort to get other blacks promoted, L.E. was on his way, too; he earned a promotion that took him back to San Antonio in late 1968. Once again, L.E. passed courses at the San Antonio Area Assessment Center for Management. Finally, fall of 1969, L.E. became the first black management employee (frame-foreman) in the San Antonio area.

One evening after work in April 1970, L.E. had pulled up in the driveway and parked his car when a neighbor approached him from across the street. In her forties, she was of dark complexion, wearing a cheap-looking long black wig, and had a wide mouth. She was a single mother of two with questionable employment who watched television and lingered on the phone.

She hopped across the street, grinning and swishing in her house shoes. She touched L.E.'s arm. "Mr. Bennett, can I speak with you for a moment?"

With a curious expression, L.E. closed the car door. "Certainly. How can I help you?"

Grinning like a schoolgirl on a first date, "Well, your children, Sharon and Kenneth, were playing with my kids earlier. I was watching them from the window. Kenneth hit my daughter, causing her to cry."

L.E. was shocked and embarrassed and asked if her child was all right and apologized for his son's bad behavior.

L.E. came storming through the front door, throwing his briefcase. He quickly greeted Essie and called for the kids.

Angrily, L.E. yelled, "All of you, get in the house, now."

The kids all ran into the living area. "Yes, Daddy?"

Essie was confused and asked L.E. what was going on. But he gave no response.

L.E. quickly grabbed Kenneth by the arm, yanking him into the main bedroom. The family followed. L.E. threw Kenneth into the closet and grabbed a leather strap. Then, pinning Kenneth against the back wall, he pulled Kenneth's leg upward by his jeans and hit him.

"Did you hit that girl across the street?"

"What? I've been home all afternoon, and she never came over to speak with me," snarled Essie.

Terrified, Kenneth puffed, "I didn't mean to Daddy. I was playing with her brother and not talking to her. She smacked me across my face with a wire." Pointing to the significant red whip mark across his face.

L.E. began to batter ten-year-old Kenneth's leg over and over again. He was repeatedly telling his son not to hit girls. How dare he do something like that and embarrass him?

Kenneth had a high-pitched blood-curdling scream. He cried, "Okay, Daddy. Okay. I'm sorry."

The family was frozen around that closet door and crying. Louis covered his mouth with both hands to stifle a scream, and Essie yelled for L.E. to stop. Lisa, a toddler, crouched in a corner, crying. Sharon trembled as she held her stomach.

Kenneth continued to scream out in pain. It was breaking everyone's heart. Sharon finally ran into that closet, grabbed, pinched, and scratched L.E. as hard as possible.

Sharon yelled, "You're mean. I hate you. I hate you."

Dumbfounded, L.E. stopped as he stumbled back a few feet, looking at his daughter, slowly glancing around at the family's faces.

"Get out of here. We'll call you for dinner," L.E. said.

Louis and Sharon gathered Kenneth and took him to his room. They hugged and comforted him. Essie rolled her eyes at L.E. and went to get Lisa out of the corner to quiet and soothe her. After everyone left the room, L.E. stood there for a few moments groaning, dropped his head, looked at the floor beneath him, and tapped his foot.

After a few minutes, Essie called the family for dinner. L.E. washed up and met the family at the kitchen table. Everyone was saddened and didn't talk other than to say their prayer and Bible verse before eating.

If the boys got into an argument, fought, or were disobedient, L.E. got a thick strap, pinned them in the closet, and wailed on their legs. This event happened twice but was so harsh that his children were traumatized, and arguments ensued between him and Essie.

What the Bennetts knew about discipline came from their parents. It was nothing short of what the old enslaver delivered. Repeated strikes with a leather belt or an extension cord in the same area. After the act, this punitive treatment damaged the skin and was painful long after— physically, psychologically, and emotionally. During a whipping, one of L.E.'s famous statements was, "I will break your leg."

How was a child supposed to respond to a parent who said they loved them but hurt them physically and emotionally? An emotional wall went up, distancing them from the parent, causing a search outside the family for closeness, love, and understanding. The offspring may turn to alcohol or drugs. They may turn to theft, self-mutilation, promiscuity, low self-esteem, etc.

You must not embarrass L.E. with bad behavior in school, neighborhood, or church. Moreover, he would believe another adult versus his children. It never occurred to L.E. that some black people may be jealous and lie to cause strife.

L.E. was goal-oriented and a pressure cooker that was bound to pop. What could Essie do? She wanted to make their home a place of comfort and serenity, but the time had come when they needed to discuss some things head-on. A few days had passed, and Essie decided to speak with L.E. after dinner, and the children had gone to bed.

It had been another busy day with work, answering a request to register to vote and plan the next NAACP meeting agenda. Then, as the family was preparing to sit down for dinner, L.E. arrived home around 6 p.m.

The kids had huge smiles on their faces. Then, as they ran to meet him, they yelled, "Daddy," except Kenneth smirked, and he hung back a bit. After that, Kenneth didn't show as much excitement, and his voice was low.

Essie smiled and went to get L.E.'s plate out of the oven. As Essie placed the dinner plate on the table in front of L.E., everyone sat back down, kissing him as she leaned over.

"Welcome home, baby."

"Thank you, sweetheart." L.E. grinned. They all joined hands, bowed heads, closed eyes, and prayed.

L.E. blessed the food, per their custom, and each person said a verse from the Bible before they ate. The house was full of the succulent aroma of Essie's cooking as the Bennett children told their daddy about their day. They spoke about their grades, playing church, tetherball, four-square at recess; their favorite books; and the latest schoolyard gossip.

When the family finished their meal, Essie told them to bathe and get ready for bed. Sharon was first, then Kenneth and Louis, respectively. They knew the protocol. Home from school and do homework first. After their homework, the children could play till dinner, bathe, or shower for bed. The boys always took showers, but Sharon didn't have that luxury. When she finished her bath, Essie prepared Sharon's hair for the next day and put on a bonnet. She would not be happy if Sharon's hair were wet.

Upon finishing Sharon's hair and putting Lisa to bed, Essie returned to their main bedroom to speak with L.E. Something had been on her mind for a few days, and she needed to get it off her chest. She disliked bothering him, but she wouldn't be able to sleep tonight if she didn't. L.E. jumped into the shower immediately after dinner, so he was in the room, reclining in bed, reading and making notes.

Essie entered their bedroom and closed the door behind her. She slowly approached the bed with her hands clasped together. "Daddy, I need to speak to you about something important. You have a few minutes?"

L.E. looked up from his books, smiling. "Sure, Twinkie. Anything for you. What's on your mind?"

Sitting on the bed next to L.E., Essie touched his leg. "I know that I said I'm always with you, but I have to speak. Do you love me?"

"Yes, of course," L.E replied, throwing the books to the side and rising to a seated position.

"What about the children? You love our children and have no regrets?"

"Essie, yes. You know that I do. So where's this coming from?" L.E. asked inquisitively.

"Well, Daddy, we can't tell that. You're gone a lot, or you're angry or unengaged."

"Twinkie, I'm trying to keep all of this ugly from you and the kids."

"It's not working, Daddy. I respect what you're doing, and our people need it. But we need you, too!

"What? But you got me, Essie."

Shaking her head with a tear down her cheek, she said, "No, mm-mmm. Sometimes, you're gone more than I expect, which is fine. But, I did agree to support you. Also, the children love time with you on weekends, but they always ask when you're coming home during the week."

L.E. began to speak, "Well, I...."

"No, I'm not finished. Let me say my piece. You're not to discipline the kids in anger again. Do you understand me? Don't believe some envious trollop from across the street ahead of your children. Calm down first. Talk to them about the situation, and we decide on the punishment together."

L.E. jumped up from the bed in disbelief. "I'm their father."

"I know who you are, and you're under tremendous pressure. But, sadly, you're taking it out on them, Daddy."

L.E. took a deep breath and exhaled sharply. "All right, I trust you, and I understand. Consider it done."

With a sigh of relief, that hurdle was over. Essie began to get up. "Thank you, Daddy."

"Essie, I have a request myself."

"Oh, what's that?" Stopping in her tracks, Essie asked in surprise.

"Sharon...she needs to go to charm school."

With her eyes widened and her hand over her chest, Essie asked, "What?"

"She's getting too old to be wrestling boys, climbing trees and buildings, and coming in with dirty, scratched legs. There is to be no more of this tomboy stuff. People are watching us, and that's unacceptable. I want you to put her in charm school."

"Sharon's not going to like that, L.E. Besides, you always encouraged her to hang out with her brothers. She's just a free spirit. It'll change in time."

"Really? And what if it doesn't?"

"We'll deal with that at that time if we need to."

"Essie, take her to charm school. And sign her up for Girl Scouts. Okay?"

"Daddy, have you thought about the additional time necessary to get her to that center? Hmph, guess I have to be the one to tell her, too?" Essie crossed her arms and walked out of the bedroom into their bathroom to shower.

Essie couldn't help but stop inside the bathroom door, looking back over her shoulder at L.E. She slammed the bathroom door and prepared for bed. She didn't speak of anything else again that night.

L.E. sat back on the bed and dropped his face into his hands. He knew Essie was upset, but L.E. couldn't believe she had slammed the door. She had never done that before. He sensed there was more behind that emotion.

Essie neared the bed upon exiting the bathroom. She knelt on the floor, said the evening prayer, pulled the cover back when finished, and got into the bed with her back to her husband. L.E. reached out and pulled Essie close to him in a firm hold.

"Honey, I'm so sorry. I realize I'm wrong. I was not aware that I was taking things out on the kids. Now, I see you're right; it's been a lot of stress and pressure. I'll never do it again. I love you, and I love my family. Please forgive me."

Essie touched L.E.s arm. "I forgive you. Children are forgiving and love us. But not if this type of thing keeps happening. Now, you must get your rest."

"Also, I wouldn't betray your trust. I need you. I love you."

"All right, L.E. Goodnight."

The civil rights movement was making significant advancements for not only black people but also Jewish, white single women, and mothers. The NAACP assisted in getting fair employment opportunities and housing for all people. The general public didn't even know that several Caucasians were founders and board members. However, there were still pockets of racism that the NAACP needed to tackle.

At home, L.E. was working on communicating positively with his children. Consequently, his civil rights and work causes had deteriorated those relationships. He desperately wanted to regain their trust. L.E. decided to take Sharon out for her 13th birthday to improve matters. He and the boys would be escorts, and L.E. would teach them proper date etiquette.

On Sunday, May 3, 1970, the children arrived excited. The boys cleaned up handsomely in their black church suits, and L.E. showed them how to shave and apply cologne. Essie had given Sharon a pretty pink dress with tulle for her birthday and put her hair up.

The black Lincoln limousine arrived right on time at 7:00 p.m. A funeral home connection of their L.E.'s. The driver came to the door, and everyone was ecstatic. Essie, who planned to rest, held Lisa and saw them off.

The boys took out, running to hop into the limo. L.E. had to call them back.

"Hey, hey, hey. Come back here. You take your date by the arm or hand and escort Sharon to the car."

L.E. presented her with flowers that Essie had quickly handed him from the fridge, and Sharon took her father's extended arm. Louis took the other side.

Smiling, L.E. said, "Kenneth, get the door for her."

Kenneth held the door open, grinning with the other hand directing the way into the car. Once inside, L.E. ensured her dress was out of the way before closing the door. He then got in the front with the chauffeur, and the boys got in the back on the other side.

L.E. continued the lesson en route to a seafood restaurant—Sharon's favorite—in downtown San Antonio.

Turning to the backseat to see his daughter's face, L.E. said, "Baby, if a guy doesn't open the door to let you in or out, you stand or sit there until he does. Also, you call me if he doesn't want to act like a gentleman. You don't have to put up with that. Never run out to a car when a guy honks the horn. He should have enough care for you to come to the door. Understood?"

"Yes, Daddy. I got it."

L.E. then looked at the boys for their confirmation, too. He put on some music for them and started a conversation with the driver about the current political climate. That was L.E., constantly checking on someone's voting status and how they were doing with their goals and plans.

Shortly, they arrived at the restaurant, and all the males hopped out and went around to Sharon's door. L.E. opened the door, and the boys stood there at attention. Then, taking her arms, they entered the restaurant, checked in, and the hostess escorted the family to their table. The children began to sit down, and L.E. stopped them.

Holding his index finger in the air, he said, "No, no. You pull your date's chair out and sit the date first."

L.E. demonstrated this for them as Sharon took her seat. Louis pulled the chair out for Kenneth, and they laughed. Then, they viewed the menu, ordered, and talked about payment. If the man invited you out, he should pay. The man is the hunter, and the woman is the prize. If a man is pursuing you, he should pay. After commitment, it's okay for the woman to pay for some things.

The family relished a joyous evening of chatting, eating, and laughing. They loved time with their father, and he loved seeing them happy. Things almost seemed reasonable again. The chauffeur picked them up outside and took the family home when the meal was over.

As they entered the house, L.E. stole a quiet moment with his daughter.

Holding her face in his hands, he told her, "Baby, you are my princess, and Daddy loves you very much. Know that I'm always here for you. So never think you have to do what some guy says to get what you need or want. Come to your mother or me. Okay?"

Sharon lightly chuckled. "Yes, Daddy. Thank you for a great birthday. It was the best."

L.E. kissed his daughter on each cheek and hugged her. "You're welcome, baby. Now, go to bed."

"Okay, night."

"Goodnight."

L.E. grinned as he headed to the boys' room. He could hear them tussling as he approached, lightly knocked on the door, and opened it. The boys were only halfway out of their suits and froze in action as they looked up to see their father enter.

L.E. chuckled and asked, "What are you clowns up to?"

They answered, "Nothing, Daddy, just playing."

"Well, I just want to holler at ya a minute."

Standing at attention, the boys were all ears. "Yes, sir."

"Look, I'm truly sorry. Daddy didn't mean to hurt you. I went a little overboard on your discipline, and I won't ever do that again. You dudes must know that I love you with all of my heart. I'm sorry!"

Louis, fourteen, and Kenneth, ten, gave a half-smile as Louis responded, and Kenneth nodded.

Louis said, "It's okay, Pops. We know that you've been working super hard. We love you, too."

"Bring it in, guys," L.E. gestured as he opened his arms to hug them. "I'm so proud of you guys. However, I won't be taking it easy on you at our next wrestling match."

He grappled with the boys for a few minutes and put some wrestling moves on them. Next, L.E. told them to finish getting ready for bed because they had school. He then said goodnight and headed on to his bedroom.

Time marched on, but inequality continued to exist. Although more significant and better homes were available, minorities still were directed to predominately black areas. Real estate steering and red-lining were rampant. Also, the economic gap between black and whites was enormous.

Moreover, L.E. had to be educated and work twice as hard to glean promotions. The underlying racism and rude remarks still occurred sporadically. L.E. had been dealing with bigotry for a long time and knew how to respond calmly, quickly, and directly, making someone feel foolish without frankly saying it.

Although the union had accomplished much, there was still much work. For example, in the 1950s, Southwestern Bell had shut down its St. Louis, Missouri, customer service office, stating they would integrate due to the civil rights movement. Though a northern state, it had been staffed entirely by Negro people since the 1940s to deal with their Negro customers. However, Bell didn't name its first woman manager of a business unit until 1966, in St. Louis (1943: First Black Operator Hired in NJ Bell).

On December 10, 1970, the U.S. Equal Employment Opportunity Commission (E.E.O.C.) filed charges against AT&T and its twenty-four operating companies for discriminating based on sex, race, and national origin in their employment practices. The specific allegations included:

1. Extreme segregation of jobs by sex. The commission found that women held almost all low-paying jobs in the Bell System.

2. Recruiting, hiring, and promotion practices that discriminated against women.

3. Lower wages paid to women than to men for equivalent jobs.

4. Exceptionally few blacks in craft jobs.

5. Very few Hispanic workers anywhere in the Bell System.

6. Minorities are grouped in the lowest-paying jobs.

The E.E.O.C. tried for two years to force AT&T to comply with the Equal Pay Act of 1963 and the Civil Rights Act of 1964. Finally, on January 18, 1973, AT&T, the E.E.O.C., the Department of Labor, and the Justice Department reached an agreement on the charges. The settlement, called the "consent decree," provided compensation for past discrimination victims and an affirmative action program for changing the pattern of discrimination in the Bell Telephone System.

The settlement included $5 million in back pay to 13,000 women and minority men and an estimated $30 million in wage adjustments for women and minority workers. On May 30, 1974, a second consent decree provided $30 million in back pay and wage adjustments to 25,000 employees in lower management positions. The Bell Systems and AT&T would merge and split several times over the decades.

In summer 1971, L.E. was a chief testboardman, going from chief to switchman in less than six months, and was the San Antonio Golden Mile Optimist club director. His community service and charity continued to be vital to him as a humanist and activist. L.E. remained active with the C.W.A. union, the NAACP, and employee rights because inequality continued.

In early 1973, L.E. became the first black first-line project engineer's supervisor in the Special Services District. His department managed complete schematics of the arena and its electronic layout for all electrical and phone services, the same for all businesses or neighborhoods in his district.

In Midsummer 1973, there was a vast wrestling show downtown at the Municipal Auditorium. L.E.'s department oversaw the event's telephone, microphone, and large screen projection services; these tasks included front row tickets for himself and his children.

L.E. got home, and Louis, Kenneth, and Sharon were jumping around and clowning all over the place. They were going to see a live wrestling show, and the weekend couldn't come quickly enough. Lisa, who had just turned six, could not have cared less about going. However, she'd gotten her to ride around town and regularly played at the park with her daddy.

One could see a lot from the front row. For example, when a wrestler hit another with a chair or a hammer, the kids could tell it wasn't complete contact. Sharon, Louis, and Kenneth munched on popcorn and sipped soda as they discussed their nuances, but it was still a great show. Once the show was over and L.E. was ready, they headed home, laughing and chattering.

At the end of summer 1973, L.E. earned another promotion as the first Black American to the second-line management position entitled Toll Methods Supervisor in Plant Operations at General Headquarters in St. Louis, Missouri, with oversight responsibility for the operation of the special services districts for Southwestern Bell Company. This position accounted for a large portion of the company's revenue.

In Missouri, L.E.'s only problem initially was that he didn't realize he needed to wear wool socks instead of silk ones to keep his feet warm. But he soon learned that it wasn't the hot south, and you didn't wear silk socks in the winter.

The three eldest children were in high school and not happy about relocating. That meant leaving their friends. The family had recently moved back from Corpus in 1968 at the end of the school year. After the initial shock of being bused to a junior high school in the heart of the east side and having to fight off bullies, the kids settled in with sports, class activities, and friends' parties. They were not pleased about moving to a cold northern state but felt they had no choice.

L.E. wanted the family to live in the suburbs north of St. Louis. It was a racially mixed neighborhood. L.E. was thrilled and couldn't wait to share a professional baseball game. So they went to see the Cardinals and Bob Gibson play. L.E. felt that aversion to people because of their skin color was wrong, and he was determined to give his family the best life he could. That included living on the north side.

L.E. made historical strides with the phone company and continued assisting qualified blacks in getting well-paid, trained positions and advancements. However, his family wasn't as pleased. The adjustment proved to be more complex than previously thought.

The children's first direct student experiences with racism in this state happened in Hazelwood, Missouri. They had moved three months into the new school year of 1973, and they started to show signs of depression in the cold country whose people outwardly despised them for the color of their skin. Little kids didn't confront them at their old school, calling them 'N,' spitting toward them, or hitting them. But, in Hazelwood, they did.

The harassment began on a small scale, with white classmates taking their supplies from art boxes or bumping them in the hallways. Of course, the Bennett children didn't tolerate bullying, but that could be a double-edged sword with trips to the principal's office.

Louis, Sharon, and Kenneth had to glean many friends, which was necessary for a racial battle. These friends would have your back. But unfortunately, non-whites who were loners made themselves easy targets.

After arriving at school, a fight turned into a riot. The sparks' exact source was unknown, but a massive battle broke out one morning in winter 1974 in front of the high schoolyard. Before long, it appeared that most students were involved, and someone called the police. It was likely because it was such a wild and chaotic scene. Students trampled across the snowy lawn, and the sound resembled a loud locust hoard, which moved from the front by the school buses across the yard toward the back. Kenneth and Louis were involved, but there were no arrests. Sharon managed to get straight to class. The teenagers didn't divulge a word to their father. He was dealing with work.

L.E. purchased a new 1974 silver Buick "deuce and a quarter" (Electra 225) for Essie and used a green 1969 Oldsmobile Cutlass Supreme for the kids to get around town.

While the boys and two of their friends were out driving one evening, they stopped at a convenience store. As the kids got back into the car, a group of white boys passed through the lot, shouting profanities, spitting, and throwing trash out of the vehicle.

Louis was so enraged that they all jumped into their car and caught up with them. Testosterone was raging, and both vehicles pulled over for the showdown. Unluckily, when it was over, the agitators fell short. One received a broken jaw, and their car got banged up with their own baseball bat.

After a few days, two police officers showed up at L.E.s front door, asking to speak to Kenneth and Louis Bennetts' parents. L.E. invited them in and asked what their visit was referencing. As far as the Bennetts were concerned, those racist agitators got what they deserved. Those teens started something they couldn't finish. Nonetheless, the police arrested the boys, and L.E. contacted an attorney.

Through this process, the representation of the boys cost L.E. and Essie a sizeable portion of their retirement fund. They received legal representation, but L.E. made a statement for his sons. The final agreement entailed payments toward the medical bills, Kenneth had to stay out of trouble, and Louis promptly went into the Air Force after high school graduation. A graduation class consisted of only five blacks; Louis and Sharon were two. As far as Sharon was concerned, the fight against disparities seemed more a negative than a positive. Neither Sharon nor Louis attended their proms and didn't participate in band or sports.

In spring 1975, L.E. was at the phone company's general headquarters in St. Louis to meet with other new young company first-line managers. Bell designed a "skip-level" session to give the younger managers a chance to gain insight from upper-level management and the company policy and advancement opportunities. Mr. Randall (Randy) Barron, the company vice president, presided over the meeting. The tables were in a U-formation, with Mr. Barron sitting upfront.

A new young white male manager, sitting next to L.E., raised his hand to question promotions. The young man believed the company skipped over white males to provide advancements to others less qualified. The man's unspoken implication was that black employees were not as skilled. Yet, he had no idea of the additional education and training those black employees obtained to get their positions.

Barron responded casually about equal opportunity when he was a district manager in Oklahoma. He didn't address the racism of the man's comment. L.E. then raised his hand to be acknowledged.

L.E. stood up, saying, "Mr. Barron, I congratulate the company for opening the window of opportunity to all her employees. Because when you were sitting at your desk in Oklahoma looking out at that panoramic view, the view for me and these women here was just like this."

L.E. then raised his clenched fist to his eye. "We didn't have any. My achieving second-line district manager directly under you and extending over five states, with ten first-line managers and multi-employees under me in my immediate office alone, hasn't been easy. I've obtained a college education and completed company courses. If this young man sitting next to me for lower-level management training has more qualifications, maybe he should be sitting where you are instead of being over here by me."

Mr. Barron nodded as he looked down at the table and played with his pen. "Well said, Mr. Bennett. Well said. Thank you for that."

At this time, Southwestern Bell, wholly owned by AT&T, had become a giant in communications. But job equalization opportunities were still developing.

In late 1975, L.E. gained promotion to San Antonio as a Special Services District Equipment Chief. He would manage an outside plant organization overseeing Federal Aviation Administration (FAA) and other data services. It extended throughout America into various foreign countries. The family prepared to move back to San Antonio again.

Pay Attention

You should be very outraged when confronted with the
ill-treatment of any people of color or culture
If you're not outraged, you're not paying attention.
It's up to each of us to make our world better.

If people don't have the compassion in their hearts to
be outraged and stand up against injustice
They're not paying attention.
If you don't feel any accountability, it will turn on you.

If you don't think it'll affect you in time,
you're not paying attention.
One must take a stand against hatred.
Show tolerance and teach tolerance
continue to seek justice.

Sharon Bennett 2019

20

The Call

After arriving in San Antonio in early 1976, L.E. went to St. Mary's to talk with Brother Kohennon, dean of the School of Business. He wanted Kohennan to know he had achieved upper management for a major company as a black man. Regrettably, L.E. received the shocking news that Dean Kohennon had passed away. L.E. regretted never sharing the story that may have lifted the dean's spirits. However, L.E. did enroll that fall to complete his bachelor's in business administration with St. Mary's.

In his career, L.E. was a force to be reckoned with in union circles and employment equality. He was known across the region as a disciplined and honest man by whites and blacks alike. Moreover, he had a reputation for standing his ground in the face of racism by whites in management. Each time bigots drew a line in the sand against L.E.'s agitation for workplace justice, he crossed it.

The fight for equal employment won for the most part. Indeed, there are still incidents across the United States that persist against people of color, primarily blacks, women, and gays. And the cases are addressed individually. But, when necessary, groups that believe in equal rights for all will rise.

L.E. would fight injustice wherever he saw it. However, he continued to serve his community while achieving his main goals. L.E. was organizing scholarship funds, participating on local boards as a president, trustee, or chairman in San Antonio, and improving the hiring, training, and operating functions of Southwestern Bell/AT&T as they related to his division.

With short notice in 1980, Southwestern Bell/AT&T established a new Field Service Assistance Bureau in northeast San Antonio with high-speed data equipment to work with the Trunks Integrated Records Keeping System (T.I.R.K.S.). There was no time for ordering new equipment or training the additional staff. L.E. went out personally to survey the job and made plans to complete the necessary circuitry moves on time without hesitation. The customer was so pleased that they wrote a letter to the company.

L.E.'s internal battle with drinking and the self-applied stress of success in everything he participated in continued. The year 1984 proved very challenging. His division hired many employees that were only semi-skilled and needed technical training to move to the skilled entry-level.

With the company's current and expected future growth, L.E. proposed constructing an on-site training center with the cost difference of not sending employees outside of AT&T for training. He designed the center's layout and developed a mini-course. According to his guidance and electrical specifications, Southwestern Bell/AT&T congratulated and approved L.E.'s plans and the mini-training complex on the second floor at 501 8th Street in San Antonio.

On February 6, 1988, L.E. and Ray visited their sister Martha's house in San Antonio for their occasional Saturday drinks and parlay. It was a beautiful sunny day, with no cloud in the sky. The weather in itself was unusual for February.

After a few hours, L.E. started home from Martha's after 1 p.m., riding Highway 35N. Suddenly, for no particular reason, he began to cry uncontrollably. He didn't understand what was happening until he reached home. Called to preach, L.E. couldn't stop crying until he confessed to Essie. Then, God imposed His will upon him without saying a word. It had been years since L.E.'s childhood vision, and he'd tried to elude his destiny. But the Lord never allowed him to get away.

L.E. began to acknowledge his call to others outwardly in his life. A tremendous load lifted from his shoulders with the open-hearted admissions. L.E. felt a breath of freedom coursing through his body. Perhaps the Apostle Paul experienced the same breath of liberty when he was knocked from his beast while on his way to persecute the Christians. Belatedly, L.E. was getting to know the joys that life had in store when he finally decided to yield to God and do his will—a precious gift that marked life's new chapter.

Upon reflection, L.E. looked back at his many decades of resistance. He thought of how stubborn he had been for years. He couldn't help but consider how, as children of our Heavenly Father, we tend not to listen— how we want to do as we please, thinking that we know it all.

L.E.'s Thought

As the people of Israel, we tend to focus on material gains
and complain about what we don't have. Instead of
being thankful, we lust for other objects. Don't take your blessings for
granted! Rather, depend and lean on the Lord. He's preparing you
for something better transition.
Lusting leads to greed. Once we acquire it, we're
left empty, incomplete, and dead.

We're happy when we receive blessings, but days
to weeks later, we complain about it.
Remember from where God has brought you. God still meets
your needs—food, shelter, clothing, and health. Remember
always to give thanks for your situation in life.

L.E. Bennett 1998

21

Answering The Call

L.E. acknowledged to Essie that he needed to call Pastor Graham of Mt. Calvary Baptist Church in San Antonio. The pastor was exuberant to hear the news. He counseled L.E. and helped him through his transition.

The pastor met with L.E. two hours weekly for a term of eight weeks. He explained church guidelines for a Christian and Bible verses to read and typical problems with congregations. They reviewed verses and their meanings during each visit. Also, Pastor Graham recommended that L.E. buy a set of concordances for his Bible studies and sermons.

However, L.E. also registered at Guadalupe College in Seguin, Texas, the first college established in 1887 for African-American students. There he continued his theology education and commenced studying for his first sermon. He was such a quick study. Moreover, his union organizing and civil rights work prepared L.E. for speaking at the pulpit before congregations.

After long hours of faith and studying, the special night finally arrived on February 21, 1988. L.E. thought he would be nervous. He flashed back to the night of high school graduation when he had attempted to sing and how his voice had cracked. But L.E. had sung robustly in the church male chorus and led songs without difficulty. Plus, he had been speaking for civil rights for years.

L.E. loved the many capacities in which he served. But preaching was a horse of a different color. He remembered his childhood revelation, how frightening it had been, and how he ran for so many years from his other destiny. Civil rights were his destiny, so he had chosen to ignore the ministry. He could have done both.

Yet, the fateful night arrived, and, oddly, L.E. didn't feel any butterflies. Maybe, he thought, the panic would arise when he walked up to the pulpit.

L.E. sat in the back office and began his meditation, awaiting his signal to emerge. He could hear the Mt. Calvary choir humming, anchored by the vibrant voices of the highly polished leads. It was an exceptional singing congregation. L.E.'s mother went to her grave, not knowing that her baby child would become one of God's preachers. Nevertheless, he had never been able to stay away from the church house. L.E. would find the nearest church no matter what town he relocated to or visited.

Suddenly, a knock at the door, and a voice said the choir was doing their last number. L.E. concluded preparations and headed for the rostrum. The walk seemed like an eternity, but L.E. soon opened the sanctuary door. The house was packed, and the other ministers rose as L.E. ascended the steps.

Pastor Graham pointed to the prominent center seat L.E. was to take behind the pulpit. But L.E. was looking out for only one face, Essie Lee's. When he spotted her in the pews, she smiled at him. With that encouragement, everything was right with the world. After the church preliminaries and Pastor Graham of Mt. Calvary Baptist Church's introduction, L.E. stepped to the pulpit. He suddenly felt an immense calm come over him. It was as though he'd been doing this for years, without fear and no nervousness. The topic was "A prisoner wrapped up in the love of the Lord" (Timothy 1:1-4).

That particular evening, L.E. felt the spirit of God holding him up. Moreover, he would be aware that his vision would continue to hold him in the following years.

L.E. was a direct and precise speaker. He set up his subject, gave three points, and then explained each with scriptural or everyday examples. He culminated the sermon in a typical Baptist manner by singing one of his preferred songs in his rich voice. Typically, it was "His Eye Is on the Sparrow." The church was rocking with glorious upbeat music. The church had an outstanding afternoon program.

His ministry father, Rev. C.M. Graham, ordained L.E. on March 20, 1988. He served as an associate minister until he was called on February 13, 1989, to pastor the Galilee Missionary Baptist Church in San Antonio.

Everything happened so fast. The whole family moved their membership to support L.E. He was proud of them. Though still serving in the Air Force, Louis made sure to join Galilee during leave. It was known as the little church with a big heart.

Everyone took part. Sharon and Kenneth sang in the choir and taught Sunday school, but there were challenges. The building was old and in need of many repairs. L.E., his officers, and the congregation planned fundraisers to make improvements. The Bennett family time stretched between work, home, and an ongoing schedule of church activities.

L.E. later reconnected with Sister Langham of the Mt. Calvary Baptist Church. She had sent for him because Rev. Langham had been ill for a long time. Unfortunately, however, L.E. could not visit before the good reverend passed.

The reverend had asked Sister Langham to convey this message on his deathbed: "Be sure to tell L.E. that if he has not started preaching, then stop playing with God. Remind L.E. that he must do what God has called him to do."

Learning of the death of a mentor and spiritual guide, L.E. was heartbroken. But, for now, he was exercising his other gift and wished that Rev. Langham had lived to see it for himself.

As he considered becoming a preacher, L.E. deemed that living life was the biggest struggle before him. A preacher must have changed from what he once was to what God had called him to be; the flock must know. Your life must be an example and light, not a stumbling block. People were not blind and naïve.

If a preacher were not living the life of a saved soldier, it would be startlingly evident to family and congregation alike. If the conviction were not present, they would have little respect for what a pastor had to say from the pulpit. People must know that a church leader's faith was genuine.

A person tested at every turn was a preacher. Making up his mind was not the sole issue. It was also about sticking to his guns because Satan would try hard to raise doubts in his mind, to convince him that he had made a mistake in choosing this preaching life.

The truth is, the church is for sinners. Good folks mostly, trying to work out their salvation. Christians are not perfect people. It's a misconception that many people have. They think the congregation should be all saved angels that mean only the best for anyone, notably their own.

Indeed, you have the older long-term members who are too old to stir up the mess and too old to care. Then you have the single adults praying to find someone soon to warm their hearts, waiting to answer their prayer. Moreover, you have young couples/singles; with children who want to lead by example and raise their children with the proper Christian fellowship standards.

You may find any combination of the above basic types at any given church on any given Sunday. However, the pimp behind the pulpit is worse if a congregation is unlucky enough. To L.E., that was the type that feels he must pray with and please as many lonely hearts as possible. That was all the better if that came with no responsibility and a free meal.

However, don't assume that everyone is prey to a pastor. Unfortunately, he is often the prey. A few church women love to sit on the front row to show more than a lady should gain a pastor's attention, treating pastors like rock stars.

These types of dynamics had taken too much of L.E.'s time. Folks made appointments for counsel and prayer but wanted something different when they arrived. The conniving lonely hearts hope that a rumor would reach the First Lady's ear, and she'd divorce her husband, leaving a clear path for them to the pastor. Growing and helping the community with their actual needs was his desire.

One might think that church members don't give time to spreading rumors. Unfortunately, they do! As the rumor mill went and the hens cackled, one such news reached Essie.

L.E.'s years as a manager with Southwestern Bell and his civil rights activities gave him the insight and tools for handling people. For example, employees came to work knowing they had a specific schedule to meet and were held accountable. Failing to meet these standards would mean certain sanctions or consequences that might affect their paychecks.

L.E. understood that pastoring a congregation was another breed of animal. Church people are free moral agents, and if they decide to stay home and sleep on Sunday morning, it is their prerogative for whatever reason. A pastor can fill the position with another available soul or do it himself. There is no such thing as calling congregates to threaten them, telling them they had better come to church in half an hour. No, all you can do in handling a Sunday school teacher, deacon, usher, or choir member is empathize with them and hope they are serious enough about their chosen work in the church to commit to the job.

During one of L.E.'s earlier periods at Southwestern Bell, as a first-line managing supervisor on the 17c Testboard and Circuit Order Group, that same situation arose in San Antonio. One individual decided that since he was African-American—a brother, he didn't have to be on time for work, as they began saying.

L.E. had not been on this supervisory job long when the man tried to test him. The first two times the man showed up late, L.E. said nothing. But on the third morning, L.E. waited for him at the door.

With his hands in the pockets of his suit pants, L.E. approached the man and asked, "Are you having a problem getting to work on time, and is there something I can do to help?"

The man shot back coolly, "I don't see any big problem with being late sometimes, and ain't no reason to get bent out of shape 'bout it."

"You have a responsibility to be on time for work," L.E. explained, fixing him with a stern look to let him know he meant business. "And if you have difficulty reporting at 8 a.m., I can change you to a shift that suits you best. But the very next time you walk into the door after 8, and you are shooting the breeze in the hallway before beginning work, I will change your shift."

From that day forward, the man was never late again.

However, the same tactics would not succeed when addressing a church worker, who may say, "Give the job to someone else." So when it came to your flock of volunteers, you had to learn how to smooth ruffled feathers in ample quantity.

Remember, these volunteers serve the Lord, working out their salvation in fear and trembling. Their payday is not here on Earth; it resides in a place called Heaven. You have to be thankful for the faithful few. L.E. dared not get on the wrong side of his devoted workers because he may not get an adequate replacement. However, at the same time, they needed to follow God's program and do the right thing. It was a delicate balance. The pastor must continuously pat some workers on the back in the church to let them know that their efforts are appreciated.

The standard Baptist pastor dresses like the average person. L.E. didn't walk the streets in the robe he wore to preach; he dressed in a suit, tie, silk socks, and dress shoes. So, it would occasionally happen that someone in public used foul language in front of L.E. or even flirted. But, of course, they were mortified and offered lots of apologies once he introduced himself as a preacher.

Galilee was a wood-framed moderate-sized church that sat off Culebra and Nineteenth street on the west side. The church had double doors at the front entrance. It had a small vestibule where patrons received programs as they entered. Once inside the church, you saw royal blue cushioned pews separated by a center aisle. Along each side, numerous stained-glass windows aligned the church.

The pulpit and choir stand was about three steps up. On each side of the centered pulpit were the musicians. Behind the choir was the baptismal pool, showcasing a parishioner's artwork of Christ.

As customary, the hosting church provided refreshments for the visiting church, and all the members spent time personally enjoying each other's company.

Located to the left of the church was a reception hall, which was the old church area. All the people gathered there, and the hens had their circle. The closer Essie got, the louder their voices were. The women acted as if a spoken indiscretion unintentionally slipped as Essie passed.

Essie was a one-of-a-kind lady. She's still kind-hearted and sweet. Essie never acted like an alley cat. She greeted the women from her old church, hugged, kissed, and wished them well—any concerns she had would go to L.E. and no one else. She wore her crown straight because she was a true Queen.

Of course, she discussed some of the rumors with L.E. at home. He assured her that no one was worthy of his time and would never have that place in his heart. L.E. was the first and only man Essie had been with since leaving high school. Moreover, Essie was still the love of his life, and she knew it.

L.E. paused during the interview, looked straight ahead firmly, removed his glasses, and responded concerning those matters. "The life of a called man of God is not an easy road to travel because temptation comes in so many beautiful packages, and it takes a made-up mind to remember what side your bread is buttered. Ministers are not perfect people; only God, whom they represent, is perfect. Nevertheless, they live by the Holy Spirit and are to conduct themselves in a manner that will reflect Godliness."

L.E. stopped drinking when he accepted the call to minister. The lives that other ministers lived that were ungodly disappointed him. He saw what Pastor Graham had counseled on about ministers and congregations.

The old folks say, "A pastor cannot expect his church home to be in order if his home is not in order." You have to take care of your business with your family at home and in the church. Please make no mistake about it. It was an uphill journey every step of the way.

Give Us Strength O'Lord

On bended knees, we should pray for our family and friends
on Earth and the Heavens above. Ask the Lord to
give you comfort, and spiritual strength,
to make it through another day. You've lost a loved one,
and it hurts deep within. But fear not!
If your family has rooted you in love, and you've
allowed God to blanket you in his spirit,
the pain will pass and
be replaced with the joy of His love! We shall meet again!

Sharon Bennett 2003

Not Appreciated-Retirement

L.E. was often called upon to visit the sick. On one particular morning, a neighbor named Mrs. Cox came to the Bennetts' home and asked Essie if L.E. could go and talk with her husband, a prior phone company employee with L.E.

L.E. arrived to find Ned Cox deathly ill with cancer. Cox tried all therapies and had only a short time to live. Extending a hand, L.E. said, "Hello, Ned. How's it hanging?"

Ned smiled as he shook L.E.'s hand. Then, he asked L.E. to sit down next to the bed.

"I'm so glad that you came," Cox said. "I wasn't sure that you would."

"Why wouldn't I?"

Ned's smile went away. He reached out and touched L.E.'s arm. "I'm sorry, not only for myself but for others who didn't believe in you. We were young, confident, and smart. Some blacks were jealous of your work promoting blacks who were too afraid to do it themselves, like me. Many did not appreciate your efforts. They wanted the pot stirred, but not by some young Johnny-come-lately. No one wanted to accept the first positions. You would have taken the fall if things were to go wrong."

"Ned, look; it's okay."

"No, it's not. Listen to me now. You changed many things for us. I might not have been able to advance and live a better life if it weren't for you. I want to tell you that before I die. Thank you!"

"Well, you're welcome, Ned. And, thank you for saying that. I appreciate it."

Before he took his leave, L.E. prayed with Ned Cox.

As L.E. exited the Cox home, he stopped dead in his tracks, overcome with emotion. Could he have been so consumed with his civil rights efforts that he was oblivious to his people's true feelings? Suddenly, overcome with emotions of anger and sadness, L.E. began to cry.

He had received a heartfelt thank-you from a non-union member. L.E. reflected on the extended time away from his own family. He drove the lonely roads from city to city to encourage union members to want a better life. Bennett belatedly found some were envious, and others were grateful for the change, but not enough to thank him.

Ned Cox was the only person to acknowledge his efforts during that period besides his union officers and NAACP members. Bennett and Randle had become lifelong friends. L.E. recalled working his tail off for the union, neglecting his family. His career got the best, and his family got the rest. And, now, he was doing the same thing with enthusiasm as a pastor.

L.E. visited their sick and married people, buried their dead, and helped them through their problems. But still, they turned on him when the opportunity presented itself.

Union man or man of God, L.E., didn't do what he did to receive glory. He did it as a tribute to God and in service to his fellow man. Because it was the right thing to do, he stood when it wasn't popular nor safe. That's what leadership is all about.

In December 1986, L.E. retired from the phone company. He had spent thirty years, without absences, helping others. He had enjoyed a successful career, ensuring that Southwestern Bell/AT&T evolved into a reliable and pioneering company that was one of the best at offering equal employment opportunities in Texas communities.

By any measure, L.E. had a successful career. As a second-level district manager under the vice-president, he served in upper management for five states, with ten district supervisors and fifty-one technicians. His organization was also responsible for installing and maintaining the 911 emergency service for San Antonio. In addition, these employees required updated training facilities; he was responsible for initiating and building the largest special services work center in the history of Southwestern Bell/ AT&T. The company would train those technicians versus paying another entity to educate and train the fresh employees at this newly designated location. L.E. selected the site, assisted by a fellow second-level manager, and laid out the floor plans for his operating forces. He worked closely with the contracting company to review the blueprints; the latest center address was 107 W. Nakoma. It is now titled A.T.&T company.

Fighting against institutionalized racism, L.E. Bennett persevered. The result was a landmark career where he enjoyed fantastic transformations in management. Also, many employees recognized L.E. as a competent, valued and respected individual.

He became active with a housing program to improve housing called the Mickeljohn Project, near his church on the northwest side of San Antonio. As chairman of the Housing Committee, L.E. worked closely with Councilwoman María Antonietta Berriozábal for WestSide Ministers Alliance community improvement. Because of L.E.'s eloquent speech, through the Micklejohn Project, according to Mrs. Berriozábal, he acquired an initial $95,000 to rehabilitate deteriorated homes in that area of town.

He was a supporter of her mayoral campaign from 1990 to 1991. He and his grandchildren, Jerrick and Sharena, appeared in a TV commercial for the mayoral campaign.

María Antonietta Berriozábal would become the first Mexican-American woman elected to the San Antonio City Council. She courageously fought for a range of progressive issues in council chambers. Her star continued to ascend after a ten-year term. Berriozábal continued her fight for social justice, serving as a mentor to young activists, clergy, and neighbors on the DREAM Act, gentrification, energy, poverty, water, and Latin rights.

Long drives were how L.E. relaxed, usually before dinner. After retirement, he began to take longer rides around town, but Essie didn't complain until a sunny day in 1989.

Finally, it was Friday, and Sharon was ready for the weekend. She arrived at her parents' home, bouncing and humming the latest tune. Per the norm, Essie was preparing dinner when Sharon landed a hug and a big kiss on her.

"Where are my babies?" Sharon grinned.

"Oh, they're in the backyard. I want to tell you something first." Essie stammered.

"What? And, why are you acting weird?" Sharon asked.

"Daddy took the kids fishing today, but there was an accident on the way back."

"What are you talking about, and why didn't I get a phone call, Mother?" Frowning, Sharon rushed to the back door.

Essie grabbed her arm and assured her they were fine. Then, the matriarch explained how her father had run his old Ford truck into a rod iron and brick column fencing at an apartment complex on their way home from the lake. The very complex where the professional basketball player George "The Ice Man" Gervin lived, near the junior high school.

Sharon stood there for a few seconds, her mouth open and eyes bulging. Then, interrupting the calm and assurance Essie gave, Sharon blurted out, "Was he drinking?"

"What? No! I don't think so."

"It never fails. Dad comes in, kisses you, and squeezes you. If he were drinking, you'd know it?"

"No, I didn't smell anything like that."

"Don't cover for him. You guys always think you're protecting us by not being open with what is happening. But that's not true, and he seems distracted."

"That's not what I'm doing, Sharon."

"Yeah, okay! What about six months ago when he was in that little Chevy Chevette? He thought he could get on the highway ahead of an eighteen-wheeler who rammed into his back. The car was totaled, and he walked away without a scratch."

"Yes, I remember. God is good."

"Mother, something is wrong. Maybe he's preoccupied or doing too much. I mean, he's never been a great driver, looking in the direction of whom he's speaking."

"Well, he'll be fine. Don't worry."

"I'm worried, and you should be too. But, look, no more driving around with the kids. After school, unless with you, they're to stay here until I arrive. So, we're going home; goodnight."

The incident blew over, and as far as Sharon knew, the kids were only in the car if their grandmother drove.

For a few years now, L.E. had spent time tracking down photos and birth origins of family history and, doing so, fascinated himself and Sharon. They spent more time discussing his civil rights activities and work during this career. It was odd that he never mentioned those racial times before. According to him, it was painful, and he didn't want to talk about himself. Nevertheless, he did what needed to be done.

Sharon began to view her father differently. But, she also found golden nuggets of history with surviving aunts, uncles, and L.E. himself. Finally, her daddy consented to an interview about his past. He responded to questions in person or by email and reviewed preliminary drafts. Questioning surviving union members, as well as the eldest Bennett, was thrilling. At the time, she thought this would make for an excellent self-published family album.

Careful of Possession

Be careful of letting hate possess you
Hate another's skin color, birth origin, clothes,
education level, sex, or success in life.
Jealousy and hate can poison you.
You may think that you're doing the right thing
and that it's noble, but hate is not usual.

You don't take a risk. You don't stand up for anyone outside of
yourself or your family. Instead, you sneak around in dark corners
complaining but risk nothing to change the circumstances.
You'll go in the same position year after year as long as you don't
get noticed by those who will harm you for wanting more.

You won't stand for a change, but you'll backstab the person who takes a
stand against hate and inequality. You dare not risk yourself, but another
can, and you'd gladly reap the benefits. You're an unappreciative slug.

Careful of being possessive of Hate.

Sharon Bennett 2019

2 3

A Parent's Heartache

L.E. had lived to see the passing of most of his siblings. Each death caused intense pain and took a part of L.E.

Kenneth was a tall and handsome young man, amiable and well dressed. He was brilliant and tested to have an I.Q. of 160. Kenneth was the third born of the Bennett children.

He lifted weights daily, ate healthy foods, and added wheat germ to his meals. He constantly desired fame and fortune but didn't have the patience to continue working a regular job to earn a high living standard. For a while, Kenneth worked for Frito-Lay and Boeing as a machinist. He later attended the Hallmark School of Aviation, making A's an honor roll. Kenneth has tried many things in life but always seemed restless and dissatisfied—more of a follower than a leader.

He showed that he had wild hair and was impatient with school studies. Possibly, this is one factor that pushed him into a dark life.

Kenneth even tried his hand at music promotions and parties. But unfortunately, the dangerous lure of the streets and drugs soon attracted him. When partying with different music groups, drugs were plentiful. An individual couldn't just have a drink and converse. People wouldn't trust you if you didn't partake in the drugs.

Criminal elements grabbed hold of Kenneth, and they beckoned him repeatedly. At the same time, Kenneth knew he had lost his way; it grieved him to think that he may have been a disappointment and embarrassment to his family. But he lost control over his life and kept getting more in-depth into dangers, and he couldn't pull himself out.

In 1991, Kenneth spent time in San Antonio with his ten-year-old nephew Jerrick, Sharon's son. They worked out, drank sodas, and talked. Later that afternoon, he returned Jerrick to Sharon and headed to see his brother, Louis, in Austin. Kenneth arrived by evening so they could talk over old times. He told Louis he was going to Houston to see a relative, but he had found trouble there before. A drug dealer told Kenneth that he would risk serious harm if he returned to Houston.

After Kenneth dropped off Jerrick at the beauty salon, he didn't get out of the car and wave at Sharon. Afterwhich, Kenneth met up with his roommate and friend from high school. The two of them robbed a prominent drug dealer in San Antonio. Afterward, Kenneth headed to Austin to visit Louis. Once his visit was complete with his brother, Kenneth went to Houston to sell those drugs. He made some drug connections in town and then attended a party in Houston's Fourth Ward without his two cousins, who had initially agreed to go out with him but couldn't due to other obligations. Kenneth went alone.

Three men tried to rob him at the party, and a fight ensued. Kenneth was a weightlifter and a good boxer. He grabbed a knife from one man, stabbing an attacker with it in the knee. As Kenneth fled the house, he was stuck with a hypodermic needle of toxic drugs. The needle ripped through his dress shirt and pierced his right side, between the third and fourth ribs.

Kenneth ran through the streets, screaming for help. But the running only sped up the drugs circulating through his system. Finally, he reached the neighboring ward, still yelling. An older man heard his cries and ran out to him. The man called 911, but it was too late. Kenneth collapsed in the older man's arms before the police and ambulance arrived.

It was early morning, before dawn, when the phone rang. A Houston funeral home director informed the Bennetts that their son, Kenneth, was dead. Nothing rivaled the anguish L.E. experienced on July 25, 1991.

After autopsy completion, the mortuary would release Kenneth's body from Houston to the family's funeral home. Unfortunately, the police didn't have the decency to call first and provide information.

Sharon had always felt she possessed a sort of a sixth sense. L.E. told her that when she was little, his mother, Anice, had told him that Sharon had the extra sense. Essie said that Sharon frequently spoke to a friend she called Ghosty. Sharon described him as a tall, friendly, gentle man whose head barely passed through the doorway.

Sharon was out with a friend the night of her brother's death. However, she decided to stay over since it was closer to school. She had an urge to talk with her brother all evening and tried several times to call him.

Just before midnight, she abruptly awakened, feeling as if her heart had stopped. Now she was desperate to speak with Kenneth. Still no answer at his apartment.

The following morning, L.E. called Sharon at her friend's home, asking her to come home. Sharon asked if Kenneth were dead. He declined to answer and asked her again to return home. Sharon asked why it couldn't wait until after class if it weren't Kenneth. L.E. insisted that he needed to talk to her in person.

Sharon hung up and told her friend, "My suspicions realized. My brother is dead. He achieved self-destruction."

Her friend tried to assure her that may not be the reason.

But when she entered the house, her prophecy was accurate. L.E. said that the mortician had approximated the time of death to be midnight.

The family's walls came tumbling down with profound devastation. The loss was unbelievable to the Bennett family, as well as unbearable. A parent never expects to outlive their child. That's not the natural order of things.

The family traveled to the funeral home once notified of the arrival of Kenneth's body. They spent time with him before the mortuary prepared the body. They were touching, hugging, and crying over his body. The morgue returned Kenneth's clothes, and the dress shirt showed the tiny rip surrounded by a stain.

The family held funeral services for mourners at the more massive Mt. Calvary Church. It was standing room only, and more people were standing outside. The community supported Rev. Dr. L.E. Bennett, and Kenneth knew many people. He had charisma and was well-liked. The family exited the church after the church services ended, crying, except for L.E. The crowd parted respectfully to allow them to enter the limousine.

As they prepared for the ride to the cemetery, L.E. urged his family, "Wipe your tears and don't let others see you cry. Not now."

Anice didn't cry in front of her children after Dan had died. Instead, she'd gone out behind the large tree in the yard. Anice stayed there for long periods at a time before returning. She told her children not to cry in front of others because they'd see them as weak.

L.E.'s family refused to stop crying.

Sharon yelled, "I don't care!"

The loss of Kenneth changed the Bennett family forever, leaving a gaping hole in their hearts. One they couldn't quickly surmount. But then, they were not unique.

No matter what her father said or how much comfort friends offered, Sharon knew that she and her children would never get over the loss. They'd only learn to struggle to live with the suffering. However, Essie and L.E. didn't get over it either. After all, they were the parents.

Moreover, L.E. felt like he had failed Kenneth. If he had understood Kenneth's plight better, how could he have helped him other than pray? Kenneth's death-haunted L.E. When people struggle with an addiction or depression, telling them to get over it and put on their big girl panties doesn't help. It takes more than flowery antidotes and Bible verses. Kenneth did go to a recovery program through a church and did well for some time before relapsing. So, what more could a parent do?

Curdell Bennett was with the Houston Police Department. He was also L.E.'s nephew, his brother Mack's son. Curdell made sure the force considered the murder of Kenneth a priority. As a result, they could soon locate and arrest the perpetrators. The men were convicted and sentenced to Huntsville State Penitentiary.

My Sweet Child

Oh, my sweet dear child,
the one I helped raise into a man, I watched as he played
ball, did his homework, or played with his siblings.

The day I first saw you filled me with immense joy and happiness,
But the day I lost you was overcome with sadness and pain.

The young boy whose eyes
glowed with promise
has now extinguished in death. The one I gave tough
love to and for whom I held high hopes.

The boy who smiled was so eager to please his father and mother.
His brilliant light is now no more.
Sleep, my sweet child, sleep. Your anguish is over.
We all miss you dearly.
The moment is impatiently awaited for when we shall all meet again

Sharon Bennett, 2000

Louis

Kenneth

Kenneth's Kinder
Graduation

Sharon

Lisa

24

Life Goes On, and Shadows Come

After the death of Kenneth, the family worked hard to pull their lives together. Depression crawled in on everyone, each not managing in their ineffective ways. However, the memory and thoughts of Kenneth recurred daily with tearful sleepless nights.

L.E. dug himself deeper into his work as a pastor and community activist. He served in many organizations and received numerous community accolades, certificates, and service awards, with rarely a moment of inactivity. However, since Ken's death, he had a hard time and often appeared inattentive or distant."

L.E. never lost his zeal for equality, politics, or community service. He spoke up straightaway. Later in 1993, an excellent example was when President Clinton was due to speak at a news conference about Somalia affairs. Unfortunately, the three main local TV stations in San Antonio didn't cover it.

L.E. was so infuriated that he wrote the stations and the local papers condemning the act. People do care about Somalia. Per his custom, the complaint was poignant, direct, and articulate. He titled it "Ignoring the President, Arrogant Move." The article appeared in the San Antonio Express-News.

After retirement from his primary employer, L.E. participated more in his church and community activities, sharply answering questions while watching one of his favorite shows, Jeopardy; after Dateline, 20/20,

60-minutes, and the news. And Sundays were saved for crossword puzzles, following church, dinner, and a quick nap.

Sharon knew her parents struggled emotionally with Kenneth's murder and needed help. Daddy's drives were more prolonged; his family hadn't seen him for extended periods, and her mother's nose was often red. But how could she get them to receive more than their prayers and church? Privacy was crucial for them. Maybe if a therapist other than one that's in the Christian circle?

L.E. hadn't drank or smoked in decades; however, the death of a child had toppled dynasties. So the truth of the matter was, how could Sharon help them in distress? In addition, how to approach the topic would be a delicate dance. On the one hand, you want to express urgency, but on the other, you want to remain tactful and not too pushy.

Through employment benefits, Sharon acquired counseling. She implored her parents to do the same via their insurance, and they did. The treatment didn't resolve all their internal pain; however, it was a start. The days, months, and years passed slowly like hard labor. But, finally, they could appreciate the simple things and find some happiness in life.

All seemed well until late 2003 when Essie expressed concern about balancing their checkbook during a phone call with her daughter. Sharon had moved to the Atlanta area by the summer of 1998. It turned out that L.E. had been sending money to every charity that requested it. Unfortunately, he had also retired from pastoring due to becoming repetitive with the points in his sermons. Essie had to make a winding motion with her index finger alerting him that he's already delivered that. He had retired from pastoring a couple of years later.

On a routine call, Sharon expressed that access to checkbooks needed to stop, and she should remove their bank cards; it was time to terminate access to the car keys from the hook next to the garage door. Essie wasn't comfortable with that because she felt it would be disrespectful to the man who provided for and protected his family.

"Mother, I understand, but your livelihood is at stake here. How will you two survive if he spends everything or a vehicular death occurs?" She urged.

Essie had agreed to remove the car keys, but she didn't. Instead, she only hid the checkbook, cards, and driver's license.

Signs of short-term forgetfulness began to show up for L.E. consistently. As time passed, L.E.'s memory loss signals crept in and took over his mind. Then, although his long-term memory was impeccable for quite some time, in 2005, a scary accident occurred. He'd gotten the car keys still hanging by the garage door and left the house. Where was he?

"KENS-5 TV News Live, the central station had to stop all trains due to a vehicle sliding down the embankment, overturning, and landing on the tracks near Gibbs Sprawl Road. One man, a local pastor, was in the car uninjured, with socks and no shoes. There was also an unopened bottle of liquor still in the bag with the receipt." the reporter stated.

Lisa notified Sharon and sent a link to the story. There L.E. was looking confused as the officers checked his eyes. The police took him to the station, but they didn't put him behind bars. He'd worked closely with the police department for community improvements, and law enforcement recognized him. Instead, they allowed L.E. to sit near a duty desk as he repeatedly dialed home. Thank goodness the phone number and address hadn't changed since 1976, and he remembered. Nonetheless, Essie declined to answer, angered and embarrassed.

To avoid numerous legal charges, a medical professional had to complete brain scans, a detailed assessment of L.E., and a psychological exam. The tests showed large amounts of white brain matter, confirming early dementia. With the short-term memory being shot, and long-term would soon wane. His actions weren't intentionally rebellious; he didn't remember that he could no longer drive or how to stay on the road. Essie removed the keys from that hook by the garage door and sold his car.

Unfortunately, with restrictions on his actions, he began to slow down and, over the next few years, progressed to Alzheimer's. However, he was still a sharp dresser and loved his hats. His favorite type became the Kango cap. The grandsons assisted in walking L.E. around the house.

This strong man no longer could do crossword puzzles, enjoy long walks, or joke in conversations. His verbal communication also decreased, but not his appetite. Instead, he ate whatever his wife prepared and still lost weight. Indeed, a lot of women would like that. Essie often said that she was baking a chocolate cake for her baby. When asked what baby? The answer was L.E., of course.

He had moments of forgetfulness that eventually led to not recognizing anyone consistently except for Essie. Occasionally, you'd see a glimmer of knowing in his eyes. A form of recognition would be present, and he'd say your name. But, as quickly as it appeared, it was gone. However, his demeanor was quiet and kind, more than before the disease.

During one of Sharon's frequent visits, she joked with her father. He loved music, so she'd do her Zumba and Michael Jackson exercises in front of him. L.E. would smile, clap and wiggle his feet as he sat in the recliner or his wheelchair nearby.

If he became too quiet or glared at the floor, she'd shout, "Daddy!"

L.E.'s eyes widened, and at times, he'd say, "Moochie Baby."

Another moment of recognition quickly dissipated.

Next, he struggled to stand or do any walking independently, leaving him to require assistance with self-care. Essie down-sized from a king bed to a queen and ordered a hospital bed arranged next to her. She read the Bible, prayed, and kissed him every night. He indeed was well-cared for; his wife ensured it.

During a time for showering, Essie needed help to get him undressed. Sharon was visiting and went in to aid her mother. While clutching his pants, L.E. complained that he couldn't remove his garments and to leave him alone because he had a wife and children.

His daughter laughed and said, "We know. That's us."

Until this devastating illness, the man had delighted in a fruitful life, nobly reaping its harvest and suffering its many agonies. So how did a brilliant mind with a photographic memory develop into Alzheimer's? But L.E. persevered as much as his body would allow him. He hung on for about another decade until finally beaten down by the disease.

Over several days in the summer of 2015, blood appeared in his urine bag, and he'd cough. The hospice nurse provided morphine and gave Essie instructions to help keep him comfortable. L.E.'s wishes were to remain home without heroic efforts. A Do Not Resuscitate order and Living Will had been in place with the couple's wishes for a while.

Wednesday evening, L.E. began to gurgle and cough up with hemoptysis. Finally, on Thursday, July 30, 2015, he expired at home with his faithful, hardworking, and longtime companion, Essie, by his side. The love of his life held him in her arms till his last breath. They were married fifty-nine years and ten months. Even now, after his death, their hearts were still intertwined. Imagine a strong love that never fades, regardless of hard times, anger or death.

The loving couple knew this day would come. But L.E. had toiled for the Lord so long that he was not afraid to be called home. Subsequently, the family was once again brokenhearted. To this day, there're still tears. Essie lost her life's love, Sharon lost her knight, and the grandchildren lost a close and loving father figure. An actual mature male, leading light and trailblazer.

He was fond of telling people, "May God bless and keep you is our family's prayer! Live each day to its fullest in good service because tomorrow is not promised."

<h1 style="text-align:center">2 5</h1>

Honors and Awards

In October 1953, the 7th Armored Division Heavy Weapons Infantry MOS 1812 certificate.

February 1968, L.E. received the NAACP Political Education Award signed by Roy Wilkins, the NAACP Executive Chairman/President; Rev. C.D. Owens, the Campaign Chairman; and W.C. Patton, the Associate Director of Voter Education. The NAACP presents the Political Education Award to individuals who served their community in line with the NAACP's mission: to secure the political, educational, social, and economic equality of rights to eliminate race-based discrimination and ensure the health and well-being of all persons. L.E. exemplified these qualities by fighting for equality at Southwestern Bell/AT&T, opening the field for blacks to bid for all job levels, including black telephone operators, and implementing voter education and registration for many across Texas.

1981 Alamo City Lions Club Association, membership certificate. One of many.

In 1983 Lion's Optimist Club President, International President's Program Award. Also, they presented L.E. with a large oil painting of a Lion

L.E. received the **Wall of Tolerance Award in 2004**, signed by Rosa Parks, and his name appears on the wall. The Wall of Tolerance is one of the Civil Rights Memorial Center exhibit areas, operated by the Southern Poverty Law Center in Montgomery, Alabama. The award reads: "National Campaign for Tolerance do hereby authorize that the name of Rev. Dr.

L.E. Bennett placed on the Wall of Tolerance honoring those who are taking a personal, public stand against hate, injustice, and intolerance, and who are leading the way toward a more just America as Founding Members of the National Campaign for Tolerance." Visitors may take the pledge and have their names added to the wall, but they do not receive an award. Unfortunately, L.E. could not make the trip to see his name on the wall. However, the museum office employee emailed Sharon a picture of it, and she'll make the trip for her father soon. The NAACP Award and Wall of Tolerance are two high honors that gave L.E. joy.

He served as secretary of the Guadalupe District Missionary Baptist Association and College, Inc., as **Chairman of the Board of Directors**. The Directors also have oversight responsibility for the Guadalupe Theological College. Guadalupe College was the first college for blacks in Texas, accepting students in 1887. Their marble cornerstone of people helpful to the college shows Rev. Dr. L.E. Bennett as chairman. **Marble Cornerstone erected.**

He served as **president of the Alamo City Lions Club** and was chairman of the Golden Mile Optimist Club. The organization has been active for over 100 years, with over 1.4 million members worldwide. Moreover, Lions dedicate themselves to helping those in need. L.E. and Essie were both involved in Lions activities.

L.E. was **a board member for the Bexar County Opportunities Industrialization Center of America (BCOICA)** and a part of the Baptist Ministers Union of San Antonio and vicinity.

October 1990, Rev. Bennett was a finalist by the **San Antonio Black Heritage Association (SABAA)**, a part of the National Black Heritage Association (BHA). This organization's vision is to help build, strengthen, and support dynamic local African-American communities. The SABAA awards honor anonymous heroes who actively support the concept within their communities, and the event was at Kelly Air Force Base NCO Club. Other nominees were David Robinson of the Spurs professional basketball team and Rev. John Rector.

On **November 8, 1990**, Mayor Lila Cockrell invited L.E. to give the **invocation before the city council meeting.** It was an honor to receive a request to provide the opening prayer for their weekly meeting. He repeated this honor a few times.

L.E. had also served as **treasurer of the WestSide Ministers Alliance of San Antonio and vice-president and president.** The organization initiated a scholarship program for graduating seniors and college students. The Ministers Alliance holds a banquet every summer, and the gifts provide money to the deserving students after the application review process, assisting deserving students to continue their education.

In **June 1991, Rev. Dr. L.E. Bennett, with Senator Eddie Bernice Johnson, spoke at the annual Westside Minister's Alliance Scholarship Banquet.** As a result, the scholarship fund developed and provided scholarships to African-American graduates of the westside churches.

March 1992, Spoke at a Public Policy Analysis class on social justice at Our Lady of the Lake University. Letter of appreciation.

In **1992**, he taught civil rights in a **Political Public Policy Analysis class at Our Lady of the Lake University**, a prestigious Catholic, private university with its main campus in San Antonio. It was founded in 1895 by the Sisters of the Congregation of Divine Providence, a religious order begun in the 18th century in Lorraine, France. L.E. had attended this university in the 1960s to earn his bachelor's degree but withdrew to take the first African-American position with Southwestern Bell. L.E. received numerous accolades from the class that he educated. He returned to complete his education.

January 1994 San Antonio Local Development Company Trustee certificate of service appreciation for 1992-1993.

October 1997, Galilee's congregation moved into its **new $100,000 sanctuary**, and the previous section of the church was the fellowship hall. It is called "The little church with a big heart" within the spiritual community.

L.E. received his degrees in **Business Administration**, a **Bachelor of Theology** in 1992, and his **Master of Theology** in 1994 from the Guadalupe Theological College.

He earned an honorary **Doctor of Divinity from Guadalupe College in 1997**.

From **1988 to 1994**, L.E. was **chairman of the ROBBED housing committee**, which stands for Residents for a Better and Beautiful Environmental Development. He was also the **chairman of the West End Neighborhood Association**. As chairman of these housing communities,

Rev. L.E. Bennett worked with **Habitat for Humanity on the Micklejohn Project.**

In January 1999, Former President George Clinton sent a letter of recognition for years of community service.

In 1999, Former Senator Ruth Jones McClendon, Houston, Texas, sent a Resolution for L.E.'s services of improvements in the community.

In **2001 The San Antonio Police Department presented L.E. with the Award** of Appreciation for his community improvement work on the West Side. The San Antonio Police Department **Task Force's objective** is to decrease crime. L.E. spoke before an organization called Communities of Public Service (COPS).

In **2004 Certificate of Special Recognition** for service to the community from Texas Senator Ciro D. Rodriguez was presented in person at a ceremony.

L.E. liked to share a philosophy that had seen him through his career. He said, "Life is a never-ending struggle until you die. A productive life is one where you help others and not just yourself. Being a pastor means being a servant to God by serving man." These are not mere words. It is how L.E. lived his life. He continued championing the underdog and bringing God's word to his fellow man for many years.

He received a **Certificate of Thanks from Voices of Civil Rights**. The document is for his story, which is now part of the Library of Congress. AARP sponsored the program, which aired on **February 12, 2005**, on the History Channel.

L.E. received a **Certificate of Appreciation from Veterans of Foreign Wars** of the United States (VFW) in **January 2005**. VFW is the largest and oldest war veterans service organization that aids and supports veterans. They presented the certificate to individuals as an expression of sincere appreciation and praise for services rendered to their community of veterans.

The **Bullock Mueseum of Texas History** opened an exhibit for August 2023 to August 2025, of Rev. Dr. L.E. Bennett for his work done in the state. Artifact donated was his typewriter and several documents.

Thank you to the San Antonio African American Community Archive and Museum (SAAACAM), particularly Mr. Kenneth Stewart-archivist for interviewing me about Rev. Bennett to add to their archives.

Thanks to the San Antonio Conservation Society for contacting me concerning adding Rev. Dr. L.E. Bennett to their archives. This is in process.

Uplift

When you uplift another, you uplift yourself.
When you inspire another, you inspire yourself.
When you motivate a community, you motivate yourself.

Sharon Bennett 2019

Early Bennett Family History

An African clan migrated to Liberia along the Ivory Coast after the rainforest north of Egypt withered away in early history. The Dan tribe welcomed them. Then, in 1842, kidnapped from the Ivory Coast while fishing with his mother for their family's meal, thirteen-year-old Azi Bounouku Dan embarked on a harrowing journey.

He was placed in chains and taken far away to an enormous building by the ocean and shackled away from his family in a dark dungeon, surrounded by numerous unknown Africans. Scarcely provided food, water, or Sun. About three moons passed before they placed the stolen Africans on a ship to America. Azi missed home and wondered when someone would come to help.

Azi, who could speak five languages, meticulously memorized his trip to return home one day. Contrary, the slave traders sold him to the Flenard family of Florida, and the Flenards sold Azi to the Grays' plantation in Kentucky in need of money. Eventually, The Gray family sold Azi to the Bennetts of Sandis, Texas, a town since dissolved. Hattie Sampson Worthy, a bi-racial Cherokee Indian, and her young son followed Azi to Texas. Azi Bounouku Dan later became John Lloyd Bennett.

John was a very dark-skinned man, slender and about 6'6" to 6'7". He wore his thick, dark wavy hair in two long braids. Regrettably, John passed away in 1936 at age 107. He never returned to his birth land again. He later became Dan Bennetts' father and grandfather of L.E. Who could have known that the seed from this enslaved person would lead to someone great?

Lighted Souls

Liken to a vast dark forest full of lush green trees, whose limbs stretch to cover the soil with shade, comes as many tiny lights, almost like gold fairy dust. But they're not fairies! They are the blessed souls sent forth by our Lord and Savior to stand in the front and guide people in the right direction. Do you look up and wish you could catch one? Then, like trying to find a lighting bug when you were a kid, the souls receive their battle assignments and locations. Malcolm X started his fight for equality for the people of Islam and, eventually, all people. His territory focused on New York and Chicago. M.L.K. focused on Georgia, Alabama, and Mississippi but would go wherever needed.

J.F.K. and R.F.K. were for all people of our Nation. Rev. Hosea Williams was the Georgia area and a supporter of Rev. King; his legacy continues with a sizeable annual feed the hungry Thanksgiving Dinner. L.E. Bennett was in Texas with the telephone company. Other leading lighted souls are Reverend Jesse Jackson, a supporter of King and the world through Rainbow/Push organizations. Today's lights are Congressmen John Lewis and Hank Johnson for Georgia, Mr. Derrick Johnson, NAACP President, Rev. Al Sharpton of New York, Senators Eddie Bernice Johnson, Senator Sheila Jackson Lee, and Julian Castro, solid advocates for Texas and all people, and Roland Martin, journalist extraordinaire. He brings us the real news for our people. The list goes on and on. We all have a baton to hold, with duties to perform large and small. We are to keep that baton tight and run the race as far as possible for as long as possible.

Sharon Bennett 2019

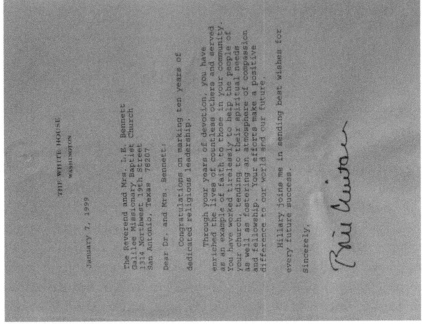

Recognition from Former President Clinton

L.E.'s article to SA Express about not covering
Clinton's News Conference on June 17, 1993

(L) L.E. in
reflective mood

L.E. and Essie
2009 (R)

Sterling Silver Coffee-Tea service set
30yr work anniversary

L.E. in a Kango hat

L.E.'s
birthday->
Sharon (L),
grandson-
Miles (Rt.)

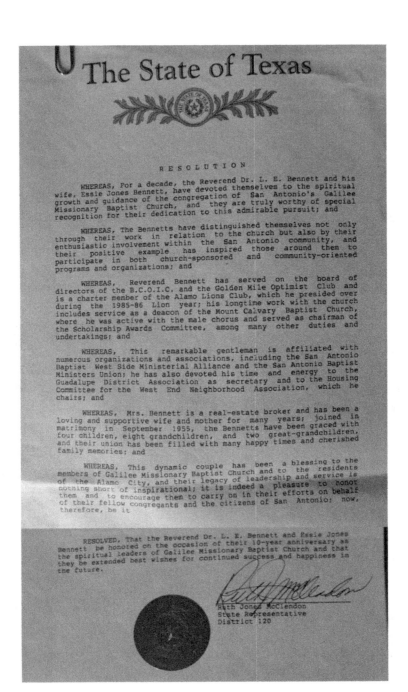

The State of Texas

R E S O L U T I O N

WHEREAS, For a decade, the Reverend Dr. L. E. Bennett and his wife, Essie Jones Bennett, have devoted themselves to the spiritual growth and guidance of the congregation of San Antonio's Galilee Missionary Baptist Church, and they are truly worthy of special recognition for their dedication to this admirable pursuit; and

WHEREAS, The Bennetts have distinguished themselves not only through their work in relation to the church but also by their enthusiastic involvement within the San Antonio community, and their positive example has inspired those around them to participate in both church-sponsored and community-oriented programs and organizations; and

WHEREAS, Reverend Bennett has served on the board of directors of the B.C.O.I.C. and the Golden Mile Optimist Club and is a charter member of the Alamo Lions Club, which he presided over during the 1985-86 Lion year; his longtime work with the church includes service as a deacon of the Mount Calvary Baptist Church, where he was active with the male chorus and served as chairman of the Scholarship Awards Committee, among many other duties and undertakings; and

WHEREAS, This remarkable gentleman is affiliated with numerous organizations and associations, including the San Antonio Baptist West Side Ministerial Alliance and the San Antonio Baptist Ministers Union; he has also devoted his time and energy to the Guadalupe District Association as secretary and to the Housing Committee for the West End Neighborhood Association, which he chairs; and

WHEREAS, Mrs. Bennett is a real-estate broker and has been a loving and supportive wife and mother for many years; joined in matrimony in September 1955, the Bennetts have been graced with four children, eight grandchildren, and two great-grandchildren, and their union has been filled with many happy times and cherished family memories; and

WHEREAS, This dynamic couple has been a blessing to the members of Galilee Missionary Baptist Church and to the residents of the Alamo City, and their legacy of leadership and service is nothing short of inspirational; it is indeed a pleasure to honor them and to encourage them to carry on in their efforts on behalf of their fellow congregants and the citizens of San Antonio; now, therefore, be it

RESOLVED, That the Reverend Dr. L. E. Bennett and Essie Jones Bennett be honored on the occasion of their 10-year anniversary as the spiritual leaders of Galilee Missionary Baptist Church and that they be extended best wishes for continued success and happiness in the future.

Ruth Jones McClendon
State Representative
District 120

Recognition from Senator Ruth Jones McClendon

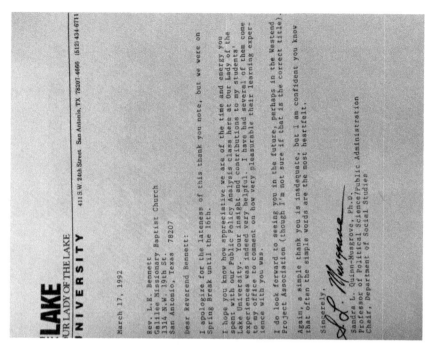

L.E. taught Political Science Class

Recognition from Senator O. Rodriguez

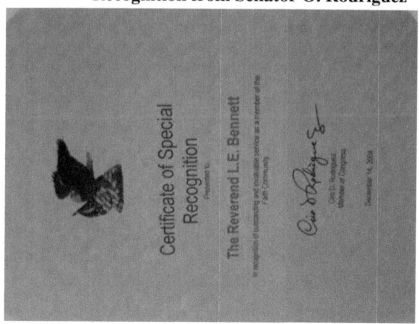

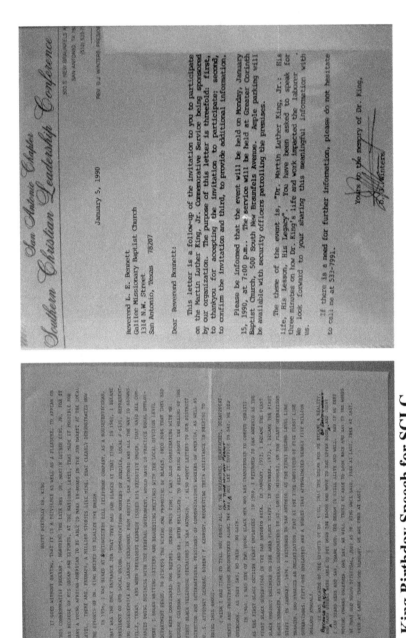

**King Birthday Speech for SCLC
at Greater Corinth Baptist Church**

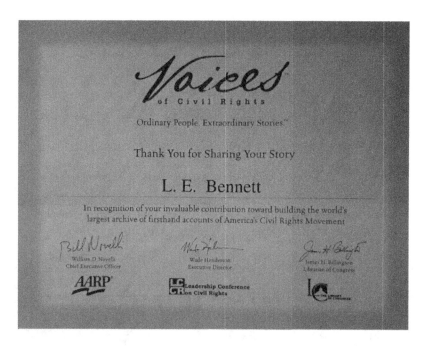

Library of Congress Voices of Civil Rights

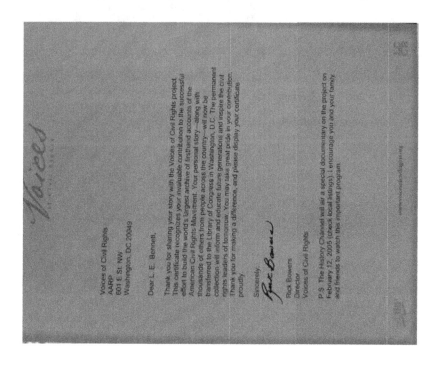

**Former councilwoman Maria
Berriozabal at L.E.'s church**

**Dr. and Mrs. Berriozabal at
L.E.'s 10yr anniversary**

Sharon and Mrs. Berriozabal

Rev. and Mrs. Bennett

Westside home revitalization project

Galilee Baptist Church
Old (now the reception hall)

Galilee Baptist Church
New 1997

Rev. C. M. Graham-Center and Rev. Dr. L.E.
Bennett-Right (grey suit), at Mt. Calvary.

Rev. C.M. Graham of Mt.
Calvary's Bapt. Church L.E.'s
father in the minister. Galilee's
Dedication Service

Bennett family supports.1st row (L-R)
Ray, Arrie (neice), Doris (Ray's wife),
Norcie, Evan (neice), and Martha

Mt. Calvary Church Choir at Galilee
Dedication

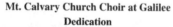

L.E. and Essie
Time and Time
Again

"We Just Need To Be Grateful That Things Are As Well As They Are."

Rev. Dr. L. E. Bennett

BULLOCK
TEXAS
STATE HISTORY
MUSEUM

Pioneering Civil Rights Leader's Story On View at the Bullock Museum

A collection of artifacts tells the story of L.E. Bennett's lifelong fight against segregation

AUGUST 1, 2023 (AUSTIN, TX) — Artifacts telling the story of San Antonio civil rights leader Reverend Dr. L.E. Bennett and the desegregation of Southwestern Bell Telephone Company are now on view at the Bullock Texas State History Museum. The artifacts are on loan from Bennett's daughter, Sharon Bennett, and his family.

"In the grand Story of Texas, it is exciting to bring personal stories to light that reflect the positive difference one dedicated and determined individual can make, overcoming the obstacles that might be set in their path," said Margaret Koch, Director of the Bullock Museum. "L.E. Bennett's story is one that we hope continues to inspire us all."

L.E. Bennett joined the Southwestern Bell Telephone Company in 1956 as a house serviceman, the company's term for janitors. This was one of the only types of jobs in the company that were open to people of color. Bennett soon joined the Communication Workers of America Colored People's Union, the segregated arm of the Communication Workers of America. Bennett was elected Chapter President in 1961 and immediately began a campaign to get Southwestern Bell to open more positions to people of color. He wrote hundreds of letters in support of employees applying to better-paying positions that were closed to them because of their race.

Despite hostility from his white counterparts in the C.W.A, Bennett continued to press for desegregation, both within Southwestern Bell and the Communication Workers of America. Bennett wrote numerous letters to national civic leaders like Martin Luther King, Jr. and then-Attorney General Robert F. Kennedy. Bennett's efforts paid off, and Southwestern Bell finally opened the better-paying jobs to people of color in 1963. Bennett took a job as a lineman that winter, after eight years of being denied a promotion, and became the first Black lineman in Texas. Despite continued discrimination and racism, Bennett rose through the company, retiring in 1986 as a manager overseeing a five-state district.

Bennett continued to serve his community after his retirement. He was ordained in the Baptist Church in 1988 and served as Pastor to the Galilee Missionary Baptist Church in San Antonio for 14 years.

Artifacts from L.E. Bennett's life currently on view include his typewriter, which he nicknamed "Old Faithful." Bennett used it during his letter writing campaigns to Southwestern Bell leadership and national civic leaders and also typed hundreds of letters for Union members seeking better jobs in the company. Also on view is a copy of a speech Bennett gave as part of a 1986 Martin Luther King, Jr. Day celebration hosted by the Southern Christian Leadership Conference.

The artifacts are on display in the Bullock Museum's third-floor Equal Rights gallery, which tells the story of Texans fighting for political, social, and economic equality in the face of immense obstacles. Bennett's daughter, Sharon, hopes the display of the artifacts will bring the story to a wider audience who might not know the story of how her father's work helped to bring about change.

"I know my father would be so pleased and appreciative that the museum felt his actions were worthy of an exhibit to honor him. Our family is proud, and our hearts are deeply touched," said Sharon Bennett, L. E. Bennett's daughter.

L.E. Bennett's typewriter and other artifacts are now on view in the Bullock Museum's third-floor gallery. For more information about the Museum, visit TheStoryofTexas.com.

# # #

Artifacts courtesy of Sharon Bennett and family.

The Bullock Museum, a division of the Texas State Preservation Board, is funded by Museum members, donors, and patrons, the Texas State History Museum Foundation, and the State of Texas.

ABOUT THE BULLOCK MUSEUM

The Bullock Texas State History Museum, a division of the State Preservation Board and an accredited institution of the American Alliance of Museums, illuminates and celebrates Texas history, people, and culture. With dynamic, award-winning exhibitions, educational programming for all ages, and an IMAX® theater with the largest screen in Texas, the Museum collaborates with more than 700 museums, libraries, archives and individuals across the world to bring the Story of Texas to life.

1800 N. CONGRESS AVE. | AUSTIN, TEXAS 78201 | (512) 936-8746 THESTORYOFTEXAS.COM

If you'd be so kind, please leave a review on Amazon.com or your site of purchase. Thank you!

235

San Antonio civil rights leader Rev. L.E. Bennett is being honored with a new exhibit at the Bullock Texas State History Museum in Austin.

▶ YouTube

Wednesday, August 9, 2023 - Update 2

Media covers news of new civil rigihts exhibit on Rev. Dr. L.E, Bennett

Aug 7, 2023 - News

New exhibit spotlights Texas civil rights leader L.E. Bennett

 Nicole Cobler

f   𝕏   in   ⌐   ✉

L.E. Bennett's typewriter, Old Faithful, on display at the Bullock Museum. Photo: Courtesy of the Bullock Texas State History Museum

A new collection telling the story of San Antonio Civil Rights leader the Rev. L.E. Bennett and his work to desegregate Southwestern Bell Telephone Co. is on display at the Bullock Texas State History Museum.

NEWS

Bullock Museum spotlights L.E. Bennett, a San Antonio civil rights leader

Inspired by a 1960 JFK speech at the Alamo, he fought employment discrimination and segregation.

 Scott Huddleston, Staff writer
Updated: Aug. 9, 2023 2:56 p.m.

    | 💬

Acknowledgements

I wrote this book in loving memory of my father, Rev. Dr. L.E. Bennett, and grandparents, Anice and Dan Bennett, and John Lloyd; without your strength in enduring slavery, the Bennett family would not have been possible. They left us a rich legacy.

I am grateful to Essie Lee Bennett and L.E. Bennett for their loving care, support, and guidance. They have always encouraged me in my writing and without ever doubting! They have consistently fed me spiritually and yielded advice through their teachings. I so admire these people of God who are a tremendous asset to their families and communities in which they serve. Thank you, Daddy and Mother, for all your memories, photos, and articles about your family and struggle.

I want to thank my many family members and friends who agreed to interviews, submitted photographs, previewed the chapters during the earlier drafts, and were always optimistic about this effort:

Thank you to my Uncle Webb Bennett for being interested and patient as a grandson who listened to great-grandpa John Lloyd Bennett's repeated stories about Africa and his journey. That gave us our legacy, which he passed on to L.E. and me, and to my cousin Thelma Bennett-Mays who helped with a few family photos. Norcie Bennett-Barnes and Martha Bennett Taylor, whom I interviewed, about my grandparents and my father's childhood. You brought them to a life full of humor.

Thank you to Donald Hollowell (famed civil rights attorney who first represented M.L.K.) and his wife Louise Hollowell, a retired English professor, for their support and encouragement. Also, for having me bring my daughter to you and speaking directly with her daughter, and encouraging her to become an attorney. She made it, and you'd be proud!

Finally, for your powerful and supportive words, they pushed me to write Jewel of the South years before your dea*th*.

Thank you to my siblings, Lisa and Louis Bennett. And to my children, this is your legacy. To the late Susan Dixon-McClenic, a truly supportive friend. To my past patients Carrie Barnes, Loretha Thompson, and Doris Beckles of Atlanta. Sorry, it took me so long.

Thanks to Aunt Bernice and the late Aunt Geneva (Tinnie), who sent e-mails or encouraged me. Also, those who've gone to heaven, Uncle Arthur (Art) Jones, Uncle Leonard, and Uncle Brother (Ollie Jones).

Thank you, Mrs. María Berriozábal, for inviting me into your home and speaking with me about my father, his humbleness, and his work in our communities.

Thank you to Mr. Lawrence Randle, the last surviving union member, who confirmed that The Colored Peoples Union #6131 existed. Mrs. Berriozabal, a former city councilwoman in district 20, and Mr. Frederick. Rucker, grandson, for pictures and interviews. To you all, I express my sincere love and appreciation. Thank you for all your support.

Thank you to *San Antonio Express-News, SNAP Community Paper*, and *El Campo Leader-News*, for granting permission to use pictures and articles about L.E.

Love, peace, and blessings,
Sharon Bennett

References/Citations

AFL-CIO .org/about-us/history. The Labor Movement and Civil Rights. Our Labor History.

Axios Austin Newspaper, Aug 7, 2023, article on the L.E. Bennett Bullock exhibit, https://www.axios.com/local/austin/2023/08/07/bullock-history-civil-rights-bennett

Britannica com The American Civil Rights Movement.

Cassedy, James Gilbert. African Americans and the American Labor Movement. Archives. Gov/ publications /prologue Magazine. Federal Records and African American History. Cassedy Summer 1997, Vol. 29, No. 2. Web. March 2019.

CWA History Communications Workers of America CWA Union org. CWA -union.org/ CWA-history/ Timeline 1947 – 1975. Internet March 2019.

CWA6300.org /history 1943: First Black Operator Hired in NJ Bell. EEOC filed suit against AT&T in 1970. Internet February 2019.

Duane Crockett of Crockett Designs for Sharon's author photos.

Eugene Coleman. Fig.SNAP Newspaper. Union Leader Cries Phony, 1963. Thank you for the old article about L.E. Bennett's response. (family photo album).

Houston Chronicle Article. Chron .com/ news/ Houston-Texas/ article and T.V. multi-outlet news and company notifications. *Phone Operator Found raped, Stabbed to Death*—Internet March 2019.

Interview with Frederick Rucker, the grandson of C.W.A. Vice President John F. Rucker, Sr., with L.E. Bennett.

Jones, Jacqueline. Black Workers Remember—the American Prospect, Prospect .org, November 30, 2000.

KLRNTV News. (2023, August 9). Wednesday, August 9, 2023 - Update 2 [Video]. YouTube. https://www.youtube.com/watch?v=TWwKXjoz1b8 Clip#2.

L. E. Bennett's Typewriter | Bullock Texas State History Museum. (n.d.). Aug 2023 to 2025. https://www.thestoryoftexas.com/discover/artifacts/l-e-bennett-typewriter.

Local .gov The African American Odyssey: A Quest for Full Citizenship The Civil Rights Era.

Local newspapers and FBI Cold Case. *FBI .gov/ news/ stories/ Houston 2008.* Diane Maxwell Jackson.

Mrs. Maria A. Berriozábal, Direct Oral Interviews and photos, retired councilwoman, mayoral candidate, and the U.S. Representative to the Inter-American Commission on Women of the Organization of American States agency and member of the U.S. Official Delegation, 2001-2019.

On March 20, 1960, multiple news outlets covered Jackie Robinson's statement about youths' peaceful protests in San Antonio, TX.

Pictures are from family albums and articles collected or taken by L.E. Bennett, and/or Sharon photos.

Racial Change on the Southern Periphery: The Case of San Antonio, Texas, 1960-1965 by Robert A. Goldberg. The Journal of Southern History

Vol. 49, No. 3 (Aug. 1983), pp. 349-374. Published By: Southern Historical Association

Southwestern Bell Telephones' history via Bell/AT&T free information Google, websites, Bell employee newspapers, Wikipedia, and L.E. Bennett.

Thanks to the San Antonio Express-News for permission to use articles/ photographs that included L.E. Bennett and the Senator in 1964; and, their article August 9, 2023 on the exhibit: https://www.expressnews.com/ news/article/le-bennett-san-antonio-civil-rights-18285422.php. Also, San Antonio Light Newspaper (now non-existent.)

Thank you, Mr. Lawrence Randle, for the recorded interview and photo in the Summer of 2019; he was a friend and treasurer of Southwestern Bell Union #6131 in the 1960s.

Thank you, Ms. Shannon Carabtree of *El Campo Leader-News,* and Connie's Studio of El Campo, TX, for the high-school graduation photo of L.E., for the 1953 article about high school graduation and permission.

The Informer and *The Register,* two local community papers, for articles on Rev. Bennett's call as pastor to Galilee and pending biography.

Thank you for family history by voice recordings and interview notes from L.E. Bennett and his siblings: Webb, Martha, Norcie, and Essie Bennett 1996-1998, 2001, 2019.

Wikipedia-org, A._Philip_Randolph.

Wikipedia-en-org, San Antonio, TX history, and demographics.